D1564391

FOLKLORE
A Study and Research Guide

WITHDRAWN

FOLKLORE
A Study and Research Guide

Jan Harold Brunvand

M. Thomas Inge, General Editor

ST. MARTIN'S PRESS / NEW YORK

Library of Congress Catalog Card Number: 75–38016
Copyright © 1976 by St. Martin's Press, Inc.
All Rights Reserved.
Manufactured in the United States of America.
09876
fedcba
For information, write: St. Martin's Press, Inc.,
175 Fifth Avenue, New York, N.Y. 10010

280052

2
5981
.B78

Contents

FOLKLORE

A Study and Research Guide

Introduction

꿩 꿩 꿩 For many who take up this guide the terms "folklore" and "research" may seem to have about as much to do with each other as "love" and "science" or "cuddle" and "computer." After all, doesn't "folklore" mean songs and stories and dances and good times? And isn't "research" that tiring grind involving test tubes, rat mazes, ink blots, charts, graphs, and probabilities? Folklore ought to be something to relax with after such hard work as research, not a topic for research. (Predictably, this kind of argument has been raised by citizens protesting government research funds for folklore, as well as by students taking folklore courses.)

However, as the legendary American daredevil long-distance

jumper Sam Patch used to announce, "Some things can be done as well as others." (Patch predated Evel Knievel by more than a century, jumping down waterfalls instead of across canyons and raging rivers, but without a motorcycle.) Folklore research in one form or another has been around even longer than that, and in the past thirty years or so it has flourished amazingly. You may find, to your own amazement, that doing research in folklore can be every bit as fascinating and rewarding in its own way as viewing, practicing, or performing folklore. It's all in how you go at it, and this book is an attempt to start you off right.

This is a guide to research in folklore for the beginner, chiefly the college undergraduate. As such, it ignores at the outset the scholarly controversies about how folklore should be defined and by what means it may be studied. As a working definition we may accept to begin with the common concept of folklore as consisting of materials in culture that are transmitted by word of mouth in "oral tradition" or by means of customary example. As a result of such transmission, folklore—whether verbal or in customary and material forms—tends to become stereotyped in style and structure, existing in many different variants that have mostly been disassociated from any specific named originator. Again in a practical sense, a valid approach to the study of these cultural traditions is through the sequence of verbatim field collecting, painstaking classification and cross-indexing, and comparative analysis leading (hopefully) to insightful interpretations; but this methodology too has lately become subject to disagreement among professional folklorists.

It is intended that this guide, by proceeding from the simpler to the more advanced, will lead the beginning student beyond these fundamentals of folklore research into contact with contemporary methods and theories in what is sometimes termed "folkloristics." In the same way, the reader may have already moved from a layperson's interest in tall tales, ghost stories, or ballad singing to reading a work like this, which is mainly about the study of folklore rather than about folk materials themselves.

Since the general popular concept of what constitutes folklore does not accord exactly with scholarly viewpoints, beginning students may find themselves confused by differences between what various writers regard as genuine folk traditions. This is true especially in the United States where many popular books and articles have discussed "folk heroes" such as Paul Bunyan or "folksingers" who write their own songs, whereas scholarly commentators have branded these same examples as spurious *fake*lore. A major point to keep in mind is that while the lay public tends to accept most "folksy" stories, songs, costumes, and the like as *folk*lore, the folklorist demands varying versions in oral circulation as a test of their validity as such. Having set this criterion of transmission, the folklorist must be willing to accept for his or her studies some traditional materials—such as those concerning sex, racial strife, or social protest—as folklore, although they are by no means "folksy," quaint, or charming.

The subject matter of folklore as scholars have viewed it includes a tremendous number and variety of types that might be roughly categorized as *folksay* (brief, nonnarrative verbal lore, i.e., proverbs and riddles), *folk literature* (folk poetry and story), *customs and beliefs* (folk behavior and credence), and *folklife* (usually material folk traditions, such as homemade quilts or log cabins). There are, of course, other ways to classify these materials (i.e., as verbal, nonverbal, and partly verbal traditions), and there are folk materials that defy easy classification (i.e., the indivisible words and music wedded together in a folksong). But a traditional approach to categories facilitates introduction.

Within the space limits imposed by the publisher, this guide attempts to touch on the research done on all the well-known kinds of folklore and to sample that concerning minor genres. Readers, as they become increasingly aware of folklore scholarship, will recognize that much of what is presented takes the form of only representative examples and broad generalizations rather than being comprehensive or detailed. Also as a practical limitation, when possible, full-length books are cited, leaving users of this guide to discover most of the voluminous folklore research in essay form on their own, using the resources of this guide and the many book-length references and bibliographies identified herein.

Besides conciseness, a linguistic limitation has been imposed here that is detrimental to a balanced introduction to folklore research; that is, most of the sources cited are in English, and many of these are by Americans. Whenever possible, English translations of works by leading foreign specialists have been referred to, although in a few cases foreign-language publications are cited as the sole reliable source and as an encouragement for students to exercise the reading knowledge of modern foreign languages acquired by many undergraduates. What this particular restriction tends to produce is a distinctly one-sided view of world folklore studies dominated and led by American scholarship, which is hardly true to the facts.

Bibliographies in most of the references cited here will lead interested readers further into non-English materials, and they should also avail themselves of such survey articles as those that appeared in the *Journal of American Folklore* issue "Folklore Research Around the World," 74 (1974), 287–460; or in the *Journal of the Folklore Institute* special issues on contemporary folklore studies in specific countries (see, e.g., 5 [1968], 111–266 with articles on research in Germany, Austria, and Switzerland).

Since many users of this guide are likely to be students in language and literature who have no academic folklore background and whose instructors may have had little or no formal training in folklore, it must be underscored here how folklore as a field for research differs in two basic ways from research in the humanities generally. First, folklore texts, unlike literary texts, exist primarily in active oral circulation, not in fixed printed versions. There are no "correct" or "original" unaltered texts in folklore research; instead, there are limitless variations created by unselfconscious repetition and from which have come the relatively few versions that folklorists have recorded. Thus, one cannot hope to pin down the *right* text of a ballad like "Barbry Allen" or a story like "Cinderella" but only to collect many variant texts for comparison. Second, folklore research must often range far beyond the formal or stylistic analysis of textual data alone to consider the *contexts* in living folk transmission of these texts and how the texts function within cultures. (Many folklore field data are not in the form of "texts" at all, but instead consist of behavioral patterns and even artifacts.) In short, the humanities student who follows this guide will sometimes be drawn out of the library and into materials, methods, and concepts of the social sciences. The instructor must decide how well this broadening may help achieve whatever goals he or she has set for the course, whether the subject be freshman composition, romanticism, the westward movement, or whatever.

Students in other fields—such as history or anthropology—who take up this guide may, by the same token, find themselves drawn somewhat more toward literary materials than they are accustomed to. Furthermore, they will have to be aware of varying uses in their fields of the term "folklore," such as "error" or "popular misconceptions" or the "verbal arts" in primitive cultures.

Ideally, all instructors who assign students to do research in folklore, and all laypersons who feel an urge to take up personal folklore studies, should receive specialized training in the subject by competent professionals. However, folklorists may no more impose a "license to practice" in their field than philosophers or journalists may in theirs. The subject matter of folklore has a very strong appeal that promises to keep the amateur spirit in research alive, although academicians do have a responsibility to point out the abuses of dilettantes and popularizers in the field. It should also be remembered that modern folklore scholarship had a strong background among amateur researchers of the last century. Some estimable studies have been made by people with little or no training in folklore, just as some deplorable works have issued from supposed specialists. Although a brief work such as this cannot hope to replace a thorough higher education in folklore, it can at least outline the field as scholars have conceived it and point the way for further explorations on the reader's own part.

Nobody reads a bibliography with much pleasure, and reducing a guide to a subject as fluid and exciting as folklore to a mere series of reading lists would be like putting sex under the microscope. Veering away from a Kinsey or Masters-and-Johnson approach, then, I have attempted insofar as possible to enliven the data with some sense of the real people who possess the folk traditions we study and of the interesting personalities of some of the practitioners of folklore research.

To orient themselves, readers should first take up Chapter 1 in which folklore research as a whole is put briefly into the context of culture and scholarship in general. (Works cited in full here are not repeated in Chapter 2.) Thereafter, they may consult the various bibliographical sections in Chapter 2 as their needs demand. Chapter 3 is a how-to guide for writing a short research paper using only the materials likely to be at hand—a sort of practical sex manual, to continue the original metaphor.

The model research paper in Chapter 3 is a somewhat shortened and reorganized version of an actual term paper written by my undergraduate student Vanna Hunter, to whom I owe special thanks for her willingness to let me revise and publish it.

CHAPTER ONE
The Subject in Context

❧ ❧ ❧ We may assume that the materials of folklore, such as traditional sayings, stories, beliefs, customs, games, and dances, have themselves been in existence as long as language and the rest of culture. Certainly, the written records from ancient times imply the presence of old and varying ideas and expressions passing from parent to child, generation to generation. The age-old storybooks of India, originally composed in Sanskrit, such as the *Panchatantra*, *The Ocean of Story*, and *Buddhist Birth-Stories*, contain plots still to be found in oral circulation. The same is true of Middle and Near Eastern works, such as the fables of Aesop and *The Arabian Nights*, and of medieval compilations drawn from older collections, such as the *Gesta Romanorum*. The *Holy Bible* is a treasure trove of traditional proverbial wisdom, mythic themes and plots, and a few secular folktales; the apocryphal books of the Bible (such as *Tobit*) are even closer to folk sources of legend and myth. Roman compilers of wondrous stories, such as Ovid and Apuleius, were forerunners of later collectors of popular delusions, wonderful providences, old wives' tales, superstitions, and other materials subsequently called folklore.

Many ancient literary classics, particularly epics, heroic lays, and sagas, set forth considerable amounts of oral folk tradition in more poetic language. The archeological record also reveals folk traditions, presenting us with graphic representations of mythic personalities and events and with the early stages of certain handicrafts and architecture, some of which remain in folk crafts and folk architecture of today. With the beginning of printing in Europe, materials certainly from the oral tradition of at least the Middle Ages found their way to preservation in such forms as jest books, collections of *exempla* (stories to illustrate sermons), books of riddles, and broadside ballad sheets.

As the Renaissance flourished, many writers, notably Chaucer and Shakespeare in English literature, drew on folk traditions; and collector-rewriters of folktales included Boccaccio and Straparola in Italian and later Perrault in French. In popular literature for the masses some veritable collections of folklore appeared (before the word even existed)—proverb books, almanacs, compilations of country dance music, works on demonology, the occult, fortune-telling, and the like.

As useful as this earlier record of folk traditions is, the beginning of actual directed research in folklore dates only from the early nineteenth century and the flowering of romantic nationalism in Europe. Prime movers were the German brothers Wilhelm and Jakob Grimm, whose first volume of *Kinder und Hausmärchen* ("Children's and Household Folktales") appeared in 1812 to delight the world's readers and inspire generations of further collectors and students of folk narratives. Some of their followers, such as P. Christian Asbjørnsen and Jørgen Moe in Norway, based their own work directly on the Grimms' method of combining the best of many collected texts of "fairy tales" into popular literary classics in their own right.

From this antiquarian tradition eventually developed such great present-day folklore archives as those in Germany, Scandinavia, and Ireland, which house hundreds of thousands of recorded examples of oral lore. A British gentleman who was interested in collecting "popular antiquities," W. J. Thoms, proposed the term "folklore" for such materials in 1846, thereby providing a name that was adopted by (among many others) the British Folklore Society, founded in 1878, and the American Folklore Society, founded in 1888. The word "folklore" has since achieved international circulation, as has the study of folklore.

The original researchers who promoted folklore studies had in mind, as the founders of the American Folklore Society stated it, to record "fast-vanishing relics" before their complete disappearance from modern culture. It was to have been a kind of rescue operation long since accomplished and the societies disbanded for lack of purpose. As it became clear that folklore was reviving, surviving, and indeed continually being born as well as dying out, attention turned to analysis along with collection. In the late nineteenth century, the Scandinavians in particular strove to turn folklore research into an orderly science and, along with the Germans and English, accepted folklore as a university subject (under various names). From these antecedents the academic study of folklore was established in the United States beginning in about the 1940s.

Folklore got its first secure toeholds in American academia at Indiana University, the University of California at Los Angeles, and the University of Pennsylvania. By 1958 a poll of American colleges and universities revealed that more than 200 of them engaged in teaching "folklore in some form or other"; the compiler of a similar 1968 study was able to generalize that "nearly every American college and university of any size offers or has plans to offer at least a course in folklore." However, full-scale graduate offerings in folklore are still relatively few, and they remain strongest in the three original programs and only a handful more.

LEADING FOLKLORE THEORIES AND SCHOLARS OF THE PAST

In setting up their research, the main question asked by the earliest folklore scholars was one of origin: "Where did these materials originate?" Later folklorists have expanded their inquiry to such questions as, "What forms does it take?" "How may these genres be classified?" "How and why do folk traditions vary?" "How do they function as a part of culture?" and "What does folklore mean?" Really the most crucial question of all is, "Why study folklore?" This may be answered quite simply, "Because it is there, an intriguing facet of culture." Whatever we learn about folklore in our research is another piece in the puzzle of how human beings acquired and developed their patterns of belief and behavior. Whether studying folklore itself or employing folklore data as an adjunct in some other approach to investigate human behavior, our central concern is broadly with human beings and their works. (It would seem, therefore, that folklore courses, if not part of an independent program, belong in departments of anthropology; historically, however, most individual courses are offered in departments of English.) Because folklore is an expressive and uninhibited means of communication, it presents a particularly promising field for humanistic and social research, one that people have only begun to explore.

Early folklore research was mainly concerned with the study of verbal texts, of folktales and folksongs in particular, and often this research had a special bias. The first folklore collector-researchers found myths, legends, tales, epics, ballads, and folksongs to be their best ammunition for the particular purpose of fostering nationalistic feelings through the romantic appeal of traditional culture. The German scholar Johann Gottfried Herder (1744–1803) advocated restoring his country's declining national culture with infusions from its great past folk traditions, especially with folk poetry. His philosophy gave strong impetus to folklore collecting in Germany and to the rise of German romantic nationalism. These factors in turn inspired similar movements elsewhere in Europe, particularly the Slavic countries, Finland, and Norway, as William A. Wilson has shown in his essay "Herder, Folklore, and Romantic Nationalism," *Journal of Popular Culture*, 6 (1973), 819–835.

Searching through world literature and lore in a rather unsystematic way for analogues to their collected texts, these first folklorists often sought to sift the traditions of different peoples in order to isolate and emphasize that which made their own national folk heritage truly unique. Conversely, another approach in early folklore scholarship was to compare world cultures in order to identify the links all people shared in common.

The growing need to assemble and categorize more useable materials for comparative analysis led to such important bibliographic projects as the *Anmerkungen* ("notes") to all the Grimm folktales, published in Leipzig in five volumes by Johannes Bolte and Georg Polívka from 1913 to 1932. The same Germanic tradition of voluminous text annotation continued in works by such later scholars as Walter Anderson, Albert Wesselski, and Kurt Ranke, and it is still represented in such thoroughly annotated books as those in the University of Chicago's "Folktales of the World" series.

A great surge of folklore collecting, particularly of folk narratives, developed in Europe in the middle and late nineteenth century. Among the most energetic field collectors whose works became standard editions of their respective countries' traditions were Aleksandr N. Afanasyev in Russia, Evald Tang Kristensen in Denmark, Emmanuel Cosquin in France, and G. O. Hyltén-Cavallius in Sweden.

Massive folklore archives grew up in many European countries. Voluminous samples of some of these archival riches have been published, but even so they represent only a fraction of the whole. A leading example of such an approach applied to folksongs is the seven-volume edition of *Danmarks gamle Folkeviser* ("Denmark's Ancient Folk Ballads") (1853–1912), prepared by Svend Gruntvig, which the American scholar Francis James Child emulated in his then-definitive compilation *The English and Scottish Popular Ballads*, 5 vols. (Boston: Houghton Mifflin, 1882–1898).

One thing every student of folklore soon learns is that practically nothing he or she finds in oral circulation is wholly new. Folk tradition constantly absorbs and reshapes material from the past. Therefore, with many similar elements of plot and theme occurring repeatedly in the collected folk traditions of widespread nations and different periods, a crux of research in folklore became the satisfactory explanation of this phenomenon. Is it due to *monogenesis,* one single origin of themes and their subsequent diffusion, or to *polygenesis,* the repeated reinvention of similar materials because of similar pscyhological or historical conditions? As early as the writings of the Grimm brothers we find the beginning of the debate between the proponents of diffusion versus polygenesis that was to rage through European and American folklore scholarship for decades. The Grimms, while admitting the possibility of polygenesis, believed that European folktales (i.e., secular, fictional, oral narratives) were "broken-down myths" disseminated by the migrations of the Indo-European peoples.

The classic confrontation between diffusionists and polygenesists came in the late nineteenth century between adherents of *solar mythology* (or the "philological school") and the *anthropological school*. The former theory, championed by the German Max Müller, professor at Oxford University, held that the names of gods and heroes in ancient European mythologies had all been derived through a "disease of language" from the Sanskrit terms for heavenly bodies, chiefly the sun. If folktales were secularized Indo-European myths, then their plots were really degenerate solar narratives that had diffused from the original Indic home. The meaning hidden in all these stories was primitive people's concern for the daily return to the heavens of the life-giving sun.

The anthropological school was led by the Scottish Oxonian and prolific Victorian man of letters Andrew Lang. He mocked Müller's theories and instead postulated cultural evolution, which paralleled the evolution of biological species described by Darwin in 1859 and was applied to cultures in E. B. Tylor's work *Primitive Culture*, 2 vols. (London: John Murray, 1871). Lang's *theory of survivals* maintained that all societies passed through the same stages of mental development with characteristic customs and beliefs developing at each level. Features of later peasant folklore could then be explained as elements surviving in oral tradition from the primitive stage of that same culture. One should, therefore, be able to find parallels for European folklore in the traditions of present-day primitives and to reconstruct the successive stages of development in peasant culture.

The ultimate research work growing out of the British anthropological approach was Sir James G. Frazer's *The Golden Bough* (London: Macmillan, 1907–1915), a world survey of mythic and legendary themes originally published in 1890 and eventually filling a dozen weighty tomes by its third revision in 1915. The most enduring aspects of Frazer's work were its influence on the poetic symbolism of T. S. Eliot's *The Waste Land* and its explication of *sympathetic magic,* or what Frazer saw as the principle of supernatural influence implicit in most primitive people's folk beliefs and superstitions.

Although neither of the extreme positions in the debate over solar mythology retains followers to the present, both diffusion and polygenesis continued to be evoked in the quest for origins of folklore. Some scholars, for instance, traced mythical heroes to actual chiefs of past eons whose life stories grew to legendary proportions as they were passed on orally; this was the view proposed by H. M. Chadwick and N. K. Chadwick in their three-volume *The Growth of Literature* (Cambridge, Eng.: University Press, 1932–1940). Another theory, set forth in Lord Raglan's *The Hero* (London: Methuen, 1936), held the opposite position, that heroes of legend and myth are completely nonhistorical, being only survivals of the gods' personae in primitive dramatic rituals performed in ancient cultures. Other myth scholars proposed dreams as the basis of fantastic characters and plots. Universal psychological patterns were seen as the basis of repeated modes of behavior and lore in folk tradition in the psychoanalytic approach to folklore begun by Sigmund Freud and carried further in C. G. Jung's theory that a "collective unconscious" has developed archetypal symbols throughout world cultures.

Speculations about the origins of narrative folksongs and the evolution of characteristic ballad style climaxed in a heated "ballad war" between American scholars for the most part. Francis B. Gummere of Harvard, author of *The Popular Ballad* (Boston: Houghton Mifflin, 1907), set forth the prevailing view of his time that European ballads originated in acts of *communal composition* by singing-dancing throngs of simple peasants, such as those who still dance together while singing ballads in the Faroe Islands. In a phrase often attributed to the Grimms, this was said to be the means by which "the people compose poetry" (*das Volk dichtet*).

An opposing theory that individuals composed each ballad and set it into circulation was proposed by others. It was most convincingly argued by Louise Pound of the University of Nebraska in numerous articles and especially in her book *Poetic Origins and the Ballad* (New York: Macmillan, 1921).

The now widely accepted term *communal re-creation* was introduced by Phillips Barry to replace Gummere's "communal composition." Barry asserted that the folk community reworked individually composed ballads as they circulated in oral tradition, so that the ballads took on characteristic formal and stylistic features bit by bit from each performance. This suggests that many Anglo-American ballads are distinctive in style not because of the manner of their composition (which we cannot observe anyway) but rather as a result of their means of transmission (which continues to shape them at each repetition).

Many other individual attempts were made by folklorists and anthropologists to formulate principles that govern oral transmission, the development of variants, and the social role of folk practices. Folklore researchers need to be conversant with certain catch phrases that have detached themselves from particular studies to become common currency in more general investigations. Arnold van Gennep's term *rites de passage,* or rituals of "passing" from one life stage to another, introduced in 1901, is still being applied not only to such primitive transition ceremonies as initiation rites and manhood ceremonials, but also to current practices associated with birthdays, graduations, weddings, funerals, and the like. The theory of *gesunkenes Kulturgut* ("debased elements of culture") introduced in 1921 by the German Hans Naumann suggested an aristocratic origin of some folk traditions that had "sunk down" to their eventual acceptance by the common people. The same term is now sometimes applied in discussions of such practices as witchcraft, once believed in by the most highly educated members of society, or as an explanation for features of folk costume that seem to preserve the high fashions of an earlier period. The Danish folklorist Axel Olrik's somewhat misnamed concept *epische Gesetze* (German, "epic laws") stated in 1908 was an attempt to formulate basic principles that shaped textual stereotyping of folktales during oral tradition. Some of Olrik's and others' "laws" of narration are still accepted in studies of word-of-mouth transmission.

By the late nineteenth century the work of an important group of northern European folklorists had turned mainly to the problem of how best to catalogue and to study comparatively the vast body of traditional folktales from the Indo-European language area that are variously known as "ordinary folktales," "fairy tales," "magic tales," or, most commonly by scholars, *Märchen.* At first, the numbers in the Grimm anthology were used for identification, or else such catchword titles as "Puss in Boots" or "The Shrewish Wife" were applied.

Different early folklorists devised their own methods of categorizing *Märchen*, but it was *Verzeichnis der Märchentypen* ("Catalogue of Folktale Types"), published by the Finn Antti Aarne in 1910 in the new series *Folklore Fellows Communications* and known as the *Type-Index*, that became accepted as the standard system. Using Aarne's tale-type numbering system, it was a relatively simple matter to store folktale variants in a systematic archive and to gather analogous tales from foreign archives or published sources that had been similarly organized. For example, "Puss in Boots," which exists all over Europe under many different local titles, is simply Type 545B in the *Type-Index;* "Cinderella" is Type 510A; and so on.

The *Type-Index* and the many published catalogues of national folktale repertories based on its system made possible the full development of the *historic-geographic method* of comparative folktale research, also known as the "Finnish method." In this approach, literary texts of a single folktale type are arranged chronologically, and collected oral texts of the tale are plotted geographically. Next, the variants are reduced to outlines of their constituent elements (characters, actions, objects, numbers, etc.), and each element is closely examined in terms of its variations and distribution pattern in order to determine the likely original form of that element. These details may finally be assembled as an "archetype," or hypothetical parent version, of the particular tale type, whose ultimate place and date of origin may be deduced from the whole body of available data.

The essential procedures of the Finnish method were set forth by Aarne's teacher Kaarle Krohn in *Die folkloristiche Arbeitsmethode* ("The Folklore Work Method," 1926). Leading practitioners of the method, besides the Finns, were the Norwegian folklorist Reidar Christiansen, the German Walter Anderson, and the Americans Archer Taylor and Stith Thompson. Thompson translated and expanded Aarne's *Type-Index* in 1928 and developed the first *Motif-Index of Folk Literature* (published from 1932 to 1936), a huge catalogue of folk narrative elements that may variously combine to form whole folk narratives. The *Motif-Index* goes beyond just Indo-European folktales and includes world oral traditions of myths, legends, and miscellaneous narratives. (Both the *Type-Index* and the *Motif-Index* were much enlarged by Thompson in their second editions, cited in Chapter 2.)

An influential dissenter from the historic-geographic approach was the Swede C. W. von Sydow, who directed attention toward individual regional variations of folktale types—the *oikotypes*—rather than to some vague historical antecedent represented by the archetype. Von Sydow also urged study of the actual oral performances of what he called "active and passive informants," that is, of storytellers themselves who pass folktales on with more or less fidelity to the versions they were orginally told.

Professors Taylor and Thompson were instrumental in establishing academic folklore studies in the United States on the European model. An international conference organized by Thompson at Indiana University in 1950 brought many specialists of international renown together to discuss folklore collecting, archiving, publishing, and study. The transcript of this meeting, *Four Symposia on Folklore* (Bloomington: Indiana University Folklore Series, no. 8, 1953) [GR40/T45],* constitutes a report on the accomplishments of past folklore scholarship at the point when an American school of folklore study was finally well established and when new theories and directions for research were just emerging. Later in 1950, Thompson spoke on "Folklore at Midcentury" before the Modern Language Association of America and traced the progress already made in collecting, archiving, advancing theories, and publishing folklore. He stressed the need to formulate a better definition of folklore, emphasized the relationship of folklore theory, method, and materials to other disciplines, and concluded on a positive note: ". . . there is so much vigor in folklore studies that we may well be optimistic about their future in the United States during the new half-century" (*Midwest Folklore*, 1 [1951], 12).

MODERN FOLKLORE THEORIES AND SCHOLARS

Although the historic-geographic method has undergone strong criticism, and folklore research has shifted away from a major concern with historical origins of folktale types, there has been continuing application of the close comparative methodology of past Germanic and Scandinavian scholarship in folklore studies of the mid-twentieth

---

* This is the Library of Congress call number for *Four Symposia on Folklore.* Hereafter a LC number will be given for each book that has been classified by the Library of Congress.

century. In Norway, Reidar Christiansen developed an extension of the *Type-Index* to classify his country's migratory legends (historical and quasi-historical narratives), which was published in *Folklore Fellows Communications* in 1958 (no. 175). Wayland D. Hand has for many years been compiling an annotated "Dictionary of American Popular Beliefs and Superstitions," a project in the tradition of such European prototypes as the standard reference work *Handwörterbuch des deutschen Aberglaubens,* 10 vols. ("Dictionary of German Superstitions"; Berlin: W. de Gruyter, 1927–1942) [GR166/B25/1927a]. Professor Kurt Ranke of Göttingen University, Germany, is general editor of a multivolume new encyclopedia of folktales, a modern international counterpart of the earlier national reference work never completed, the *Handwörterbuch des deutschen Märchens,* 2 vols. ("Dictionary of German Folktales"; Berlin: W. de Gruyter, 1930–1940) [GR166/M26].

The Finnish method, although originally intended for European folktale studies, has been applied to other genres. Archer Taylor demonstrated its applicability to ballads in a study of the Anglo-Scandinavian ballad complex of *Edward and Sven i Rosengård* (Child number 13,* Chicago: University of Chicago Press, 1931) [PR1968/E38/T3]. Paul Brewster applied the same method to the ballad "The Two Sisters" (Child number 10, *Folklore Fellows Communications,* no. 147, 1953); and Holger Olof Nygard made a most detailed and ambitious historic-geographic study of numerous variants of the ballad Child titled "Lady Isabel and the Elf Knight" (Child number 4, *Folklore Fellows Communications,* no. 169, 1958). Two Finnish scholars have published studies in German using the historic-geographic method on a riddle and a folk saying, and Elsa E. Haavio of Finland used the method for a study of a folk game in her work *The Game of Rich and Poor (Folklore Fellows Communications,* no. 100, 1932). Stith Thompson has been the only scholar to use the Finnish method on a North American Indian folktale, one called "The Star Husband," *Studia Septentrionalia,* 4 (1953), 93–163.

Many of Stith Thompson's students contributed to oral narrative type and motif indexing and to historic-geographic analysis through their graduate research at Indiana University. All these projects went

---

* The Child number refers to the number given a ballad in Francis James Child's collection, *The English and Scottish Popular Ballads.*

into the revised editions of the *Type-Index* and the *Motif-Index*. Two doctoral studies of special importance were published separately: Ernest W. Baughman's *Type and Motif-Index of the Folktales of England and North America* (Bloomington: Indiana University Folklore Series, no. 20, 1966) [GR67/B3], and Warren E. Roberts' study of Type 480, "The Kind and the Unkind Girls" (published as a supplement to the folktale research journal *Fabula* in 1958).

Graduate folklore training in the United States developed also at the University of Pennsylvania, where MacEdward Leach furthered the literary-aesthetic approach to ballads. This was the heritage of Child's work, which established the classic canon of Anglo-American ballads. Here Tristram P. Coffin prepared an invaluable bibliographic catalogue of the numerous variants of Child ballads collected in America, and G. Malcolm Laws devised indexes for the British broadside and native ballads in America. (All three indexes were published by the American Folklore Society.) Works of these and other leading American ballad scholars are discussed in Chapter 2.

The music of Anglo-American ballads and folksongs, much neglected by most past scholars except Phillips Barry and Cecil J. Sharp, began to receive more attention in the studies of such folklorists as George Herzog, Charles Seeger, and especially Bertrand Bronson. Bronson is now analyzing the music of Child ballads in great detail, just as their nineteenth-century editor did the texts. Having abandoned unprovable hypotheses about who composed ballads, contemporary scholars have turned to studies of known ballad composers, such as Edward D. Ives's *Larry Gorman: The Man Who Made the Songs* (Bloomington: Indiana University Press, 1964) [ML 410/G 645/I 9], which fully delineates a Maine woods poet, and to studies of folksingers' repertoires and styles, such as *A Singer and Her Songs: Almeda Riddle's Book of Ballads*, edited by Roger D. Abrahams (Baton Rouge: Louisiana State University Press, 1970) [ML 420/R 53/A 3].

Child had assumed with most others of his generation that traditional ballad singing was practically dead in England and nonexistent in the New World. He confined his "collecting" to printing a few texts sent to him by correspondents and either ignored or was unaware of other forms of folksong. A turnabout in American research came with the revelation of living folksinging traditions in the United States. The young Texan John A. Lomax began to publish

Cowboy Songs and Other Frontier Ballads (1910; rev. and enlarged ed. New York: Macmillan, 1938) [PS595/C6L6] and to expose the rich native tradition of folksong. At about the same time, the established English collector Cecil J. Sharp discovered during a visit to the United States a living strain of imported folksong that he published in *English Folksongs from the Southern Appalachians*, 2 vols. (New York: Oxford University Press, 1917; rev. eds. 1932, 1952) [M1629/S53/E6]. Following these pioneer works a host of regional collectors—H. M. Belden in Missouri, George Korson among Eastern coal miners, Emelyn E. Gardner and Geraldine J. Chickering in Michigan, Lester Hubbard in Utah, and many others—brought in huge sheaves of material. John Lomax's persistent urging that native American folk music be preserved led eventually to the establishment of the Folk Song Archive in the Library of Congress, which got a solid footing through energetic early work by Robert W. Gordon, Alan Lomax, Benjamin A. Botkin, Duncan Emrich, and others.

New World regional folklore collecting flowered later than the great European efforts of the nineteenth century and finally came into its own in the 1920s, 1930s, and 1940s, when such important folk groups as the Germans of Pennsylvania, the Mexicans of the Southwest, the Mormons of Utah, the blacks of the South, and the mountaineers of the Ozark region were tapped. Some notable regional American collectors were college professors, such as Frank C. Brown in North Carolina, who made a vast collection that was a mere sidelight to his regular teaching and administrative roles. Others like Harry Hyatt of Adams County, Illinois, and Ozarker Vance Randolph (America's most prolific folklore collector) operated completely outside of academe.

In Canada, under the longtime leadership of C. Marius Barbeau, folklore studies have gone on almost as long as in the United States, although at first the greatest attention was given to the Eastern provinces. Here such collectors as W. Roy Mackenzie, Elizabeth B. Greenleaf, Grace Y. Mansfield, and Helen Creighton all published the folksong riches of their country in many works. Recently, the fieldwork projects sponsored by the Canadian Centre for Folk Culture Studies at the National Museum of Man in Ottawa have greatly expanded the scope of folklore research, particularly among Canada's diverse ethnic and immigrant groups.

The ideal combination of diligent collecting coupled with thorough analysis was often lacking in New World regional studies. However, in England, where folklore research had lapsed somewhat into dilettantism since the great days of Andrew Lang and his contemporaries, good examples of the revival of professional folklore research are found in Peter Opie and Iona Opie's books, beginning with *The Lore and Language of Schoolchildren* (New York: Oxford University Press, 1959) [GR475/O67]. In most European countries, folklore research has either been continuously active for generations or was solidly established recently, but few of the results of this scholarship have appeared in the English language. (Some exceptions are cited in Chapter 2.)

When Stith Thompson retired in 1957, he was replaced at Indiana University by Richard M. Dorson, a veritable superstar folklorist, who demonstrated his abilities as fieldworker and scholar in an impressive and voluminous series of studies. Dorson greatly influenced the American folklore scene through his students and as editor of the *Journal of American Folklore* (1959–1963) and president of the American Folklore Society (1967–1968). Dorson's textbook *American Folklore* (Chicago: University of Chicago Press, 1959) [GR105/D65] was the first comprehensive scholarly survey of the subject; it took an historical perspective and covered colonial through modern folklore, including frontier humor, regional and immigrant folklore, folk heroes, and black oral traditions.

In "A Theory for American Folklore: A Symposium," *Journal of American Folklore,* 72 (1959), 197–242, Dorson articulated his convictions that were implicit in the textbook: ". . . students of American folklore must find common theoretical ground if they aspire to be more than random collectors or public entertainers. To reach such ground they will need training equally in the science of folklore and in the history of American civilization." Reviewing this "hemispheric" theory (as he calls it) in his American Folklore Society presidential address of 1968 (published in *Journal of American Folklore,* 82 [1969], 226–244), Dorson asserted that even if the publication of his theory had only "created about as much impact as a cherry blossom dropped from the summit of Mount Fuji onto a snowbank at the foot," an impressive group of recent books by younger American folklorists had nevertheless demonstrated that the theory could "claim them as true American folklorists who perceive the intimate bonds between the culture of the folk and the history of the American experience."

In addition to having been a strong force in shaping studies of American folklore for the past twenty years, Dorson has been active in bringing about what may be termed a new internationalism or cross-culturalism in American folkloristics. The Indiana University Folklore Institute, which convened only once every four years up to 1962, became a permanent teaching and research organization thereafter, attracting increasing numbers of foreign students and guest lecturers. The journal *Midwest Folklore,* itself the successor of *Hoosier Folklore,* was replaced at Indiana University in 1964 by the *Journal of the Folklore Institute,* a major research periodical with an international scope. Dorson himself has done research in Japan and in Great Britain and has published his results in *Folk Legends of Japan* (Tokyo: Charles E. Tuttle, 1962) and *The British Folklorists* (Chicago: University of Chicago Press, 1968) [GR50/D63], and he has spearheaded new studies in African folklore with his collection *African Folklore* (Bloomington: Indiana University Press, 1972) [GR350/D76]. He is general editor for the ongoing "Folktales of the World" series, for which specialists from many countries each prepare an annotated edition of representative oral stories in reliable English translations that are free of the cuteness and whimsy of typical "fairy tale" anthologies.

Others, too, have fostered an international perspective in their work despite the general emphasis for decades on regional native American folklore. Some who have done important fieldwork in the United States have, like Alan Lomax, also collected much abroad; others, such as Paul G. Brewster, have written comparative studies of American materials that are rich with references to foreign analogues. Albert B. Lord did the major research on Yugoslav minstrel songs, published in *The Singer of Tales* (Cambridge, Mass.: Harvard University Press, 1960) [PN1303/L62]. This work led to theories about Homeric formula composition of epic poetry and inspired later American scholars to apply an oral-formula approach to both English ballads and Southern black church sermons. Francis Lee Utley, a biblical and medieval scholar as well as a folklorist and onomastician (student of name lore), did a great deal through his studies to promote an international viewpoint. The Hungarian folklorist Linda Dégh, at Indiana University since 1963, gives her students and colleagues insights into Eastern European folklore research methods through her teaching, publications, and the recent translation of her major earlier work, *Folktales and Society* (1962; English ed. Bloomington: Indiana University Press, 1969) [GR158/D4253].

The field of Latin American folklore has been rendered more easily available to North Americans by the annual bibliographies started by Ralph Steele Boggs in *Southern Folklore Quarterly* and continued by Américo Paredes and Merle Simmons. A few North American folklorists, such as Juan B. Rael, Aurelio M. Espinosa and his son Aurelio, Jr., Américo Paredes, Stanley L. Robe, and Terrence L. Hansen, have specialized in studies of Central and South American folklore, but it was not until the publication of an English translation of the leading Brazilian folklorist Paulo de Carvalho-Neto's *Concepto de Folklore* (1956; English ed., *The Concept of Folklore*, Coral Gables, Fla.: University of Miami Press, 1971) [GR40/C3813] that a major theoretical work from Latin America was available to those not fluent in one of its languages.

From the earliest days of their studies, American folklorists have had to become familiar with the European publications in the field, especially with German and Scandinavian reference works, which are the very basis of the discipline. It is more common now than in years past for folklore scholars from Europe to come to the United States in person, as Cecil Sharp did decades ago. Among European folklorists who have taught and lectured in the United States recently are Reidar Christiansen of Norway, Mihai Pop of Romania, Lutz Röhrich of Germany, and Robert Wildhaber of Switzerland.

In the same period that American folklorists were beginning to unearth the genuine richness of their country's folklore, journalists, juvenile writers, and publicists were feeding the public's fascination with such traditions by creating a series of ersatz native hero legends that spun long imaginary adventures from a thin basis of oral traditions or from none at all. For the unavoidable Paul Bunyan tales (only hinted at in genuine logger folklore) Dorson coined the term "fakelore," and it applies equally well to the adventures of Pecos Bill, Joe Magarac, Bowleg Bill, and many other publicized figures.

A genuine American folk hero type is the real local character who boosts himself in his neighbor's eyes through telling fanciful tall tales that he has drawn from oral tradition and retold in the first person. Such figures—unknown to a wider audience—have been described in regional folklore studies such as William Hugh Jansen's Indiana University doctoral dissertation on Abraham "Oregon" Smith, a local liar of southern Indiana. An ethnic group hero (Gregorio Cortez, Mexican-American) has been discussed by Américo Paredes *"With His Pistol in His Hand": A Border Ballad and Its Hero* (Austin: University of Texas Press, 1958) [PQ7297/A1C63]. John Henry, the black American folk hero, has been the subject of two studies, Guy B. Johnson, *John Henry, Tracking Down a Negro Legend* (Chapel Hill: University of North Carolina Press, 1929) [PS461/J6J6], and Louis W. Chappel, *John Henry: A Folk-Lore Study* (Jena, Germany, 1933; rpt. Port Washington, N.Y.: Kennikat Press, 1968) [PS461/J6C5/1968]. The rather uneven studies of frontier heroes (Davy Crockett, Mike Fink, Johnny Appleseed, etc.) and of outlaw heroes (Jesse James, Billy the Kid, etc.) are reviewed by Richard Dorson in Chapter 5 and in the bibliographical notes of *American Folklore*.

The enormous popularity of B. A. Botkin's anthology *A Treasury of American Folklore* (New York: Crown, 1944) [GR105/B58] and the long series of folksy collections by Botkin and others that followed did much to fan the spark of early popular interest in folklore into a roaring blaze during the next decades. Unfortunately, in most of these anthologies, fakelore hero tales and other literary imitations of folklore are mixed indiscriminately with oral traditions so that the public has been badly misled about what constitutes authentic American folklore. Stanley Edgar Hyman, a sharp critic of such publications, referred to them as "bankrupt treasuries."

The popular appeal of early professional folksingers like Burl Ives and Pete Seeger in the 1940s developed into the landslide "folksong revival" of the 1950s and 1960s that departed wildly from any real concern for oral-traditional material. Well-rehearsed singing groups of "citybillies" wearing modish costumes, singing contrived "protest songs," appearing on television extravaganzas, and evolving hybrid types of music such as "folk rock" may be interesting manifestations of popular culture, but they are largely irrelevant to the study of folklore.

The European counterpart of fakelore is found in such items as recently adopted "national costumes"; genuine past folk costumes were always regional or sectarian and never distributed neatly within exact modern political boundaries. One may experience both genuine and contrived traditions in visits to typical European open-air museums. Here one is often treated to a folk show aimed at tourists and produced by professional entertainers rather than folk performers, while at the same time one is surrounded by examples of authentic folk architecture reconstructed by folklife specialists.

Contemporary American folklorists have moved from mere criticism of contrived fakelore and rejection of mass culture to a widening of their studies to take in certain traditional aspects of the modern and urban world. In an issue of the *Journal of American Folklore* devoted to "The Urban Experience and Folk Tradition" (83 [1970], 115–270), five papers from a symposium held at Wayne State University, Detroit, are presented along with transcripts of the floor discussions. A statement by Richard Dorson following the comments on his own paper "Is There a Folk in the City?" suggests how a number of his contemporaries have restructured their concepts of the field of folklore: "I am not so sure . . . that we can, or need to, separate a pure folk tradition of peasant culture from the pseudofolk products depicting and memorializing that culture. My own thinking now turns to the 'unofficial' culture rather than remnants of peasant culture. How we distinguish the official from the unofficial culture is a theoretical problem of its own."

Hermann Bausinger of Tübingen University, Germany, refers to "Folk Culture in the Technical World" (*Volkskultur in der technischen Welt;* Stuttgart: W. Kohlhammer, 1961) [HN450/B3] and casts his eye over both the mass culture that is reflected in folk traditions and the mass adoption of elements taken from folklore itself. American folklorist Ray B. Browne devotes his work now completely to studies of popular culture; he has established a "Center for the Study of Popular Culture" at Bowling Green University, Ohio, and initiated an ambitious publications series there that includes the *Journal of Popular Culture* (1967 f.) in which a few important folk-pop studies have appeared among many papers of no value to folklore studies.

Studies of traditional backgrounds of commercial country and western music, which now appear quite frequently in folklore journals, were urged upon American folklorists in the 1965 "Hillbilly Issue" of the *Journal of American Folklore,* coedited by John Greenway and D. K. Wilgus. A major resource center for such studies is the John Edwards Memorial Foundation incorporated in 1962 and housed in the Folklore and Mythology Center of the University of California at Los Angeles. The neglected subject of sexual folklore was acknowledged in a panel at the 1960 American Folklore Society meeting, "Folk Literature and the Obscene" (published 1962 in the *Journal of American Folklore*). Since then all barriers have fallen. In recent years, urban jokes and blues, the drug culture, graffiti, rock music, women's liberation, factory lore, and television advertising are only a few of the subjects whose folk aspects have been treated in professional folklorists' published research.

Whereas in Europe folklore has long been linked with ethnography (study of material traditions), the American approach in the past was mainly a literary one oriented to verbal texts. It is true that we have some notable folk museums—such as the Farmers Museum of Cooperstown, New York, and Old Sturbridge Village, Massachusetts—but these have been more the products of historical than folklore research. The "Index of American Design" project of the 1930s (now housed in the National Gallery of Art) documented much folk art, but the work failed to clearly distinguish *folk* from early *popular* arts, and it too was organized by nonfolklorists.

Lately, the Scandinavian *folk-liv* movement, which has spread throughout Europe, has sparked a new burst of interest in Great Britain and the United States in the form of "folklife" study or a "folk-cultural" approach. In Great Britain, scholars including E. Estyn Evans, Stewart Sanderson, and Geraint Jenkins have published folklife studies in books and in such journals as *Folk Life, Scottish Studies,* and *Ulster Folk Life.* In the United States, we have important folklife studies such as those by Austin Fife (Mormon hay derricks), Don Yoder (sectarian costume and folk foods), Warren Roberts and Henry Glassie (log construction), Roger Welsch (sod houses), and Michael Owen Jones (traditional chair making and the aesthetics of folk art), to identify but a few scholars and samples of their work. The American Folklore Society appointed a folklife committee in 1965, and today folklore and folklife are an inseparable pair in American folklore studies.

Methodological advances in modern folklore study, naturally enough, have been considerable since the days in which fieldworkers went armed with only notebooks, sketchpads, index cards, and pencils. The tape recorder has become an indispensable tool, and motion pictures have become widely recognized as a documentary medium; in fact, showings of new folklore films have become a regular part of professional meetings. D. K. Wilgus and others have argued for the importance of commercial disc recordings as documents of folk music to supplement printed publications. Bertrand Bronson has demonstrated the value of the computer in technical analysis of folk music. Microfilm, duplicating machines, and updated filing and retrieval systems now aid the archivist, although we still lack sufficiently interchangeable classifications of generally used folklore types to facilitate easy cross-references between different archives.

European folklorists have long employed folklore handbooks as fieldguides, archiving manuals, or textbooks. These include Reidar Christiansen's *Norske Folkeminne* (Oslo: Noisk Folkeminnelag, 1925), Inger M. Boberg's *Dansk Folketradition* (Munksgaard, Denmark: Danmarks Folkeminder, 1962), Mihai Pop's Romanian *Indreptar pentru Culegerea Folklorului* ("Guide for Collectors of Folklore") (Bucharest: Comitetulde Stat Pentru Cultură şi Artă, 1967), and especially important for us, because it is both very complete and in English, Séan Ó Súilleabháin's *A Handbook for Irish Folklore* (Dublin: Irish Folklore Commission, 1942).

Attempts to fill this same need for handbooks in the United States were made by Martha Warren Beckwith, *Folklore in America: Its Scope and Method* (Poughkeepsie, N.Y.: Publications of the Folklore Foundation, Vassar College, 1931) [GR105/B4], and Levette J. Davidson, *A Guide to American Folklore* (Denver: University of Denver Press, 1951) [GR105/D3]. However, both books are too short, sketchy, and now outdated to suffice. Many other teachers, researchers, and regional folklore societies compiled their own surveys and guides for private use, but as a whole the only worthy counterparts to the European handbooks that American folklorists can rely on are Kenneth S. Goldstein's *A Guide for Field Workers in Folklore* (Hatboro, Pa.: American Folklore Society, 1964) and several other basic works of the past ten years, including Jan Harold Brunvand's

The Study of American Folklore: An Introduction (New York: W. W. Norton, 1968).

New approaches to analysis in folklore studies generally develop in a sequence from collection to classification to interpretation, although it should be remembered that none of these stages is ever abandoned, that not all folklorists necessarily engage in all three, and that the best fieldwork and archiving efforts also require a sound theoretical background. Studies of folk games in the United States serve as good examples of changing techniques. They began with efforts such as W. W. Newell's romanticized collections of singing games in the 1880s (based on nineteenth-century English studies). Then they progressed through the systematic annotations and classifications of Paul Brewster and others in the 1940s. Today, studies of folk games are represented in such sophisticated works of analysis as those of Brian Sutton-Smith, who has characterized his approach as "multilevel historical, sociological, psychological and ludic [play element] analysis."

Some of the most widely accepted twentieth-century modes of folklore analysis have developed out of established approaches of the past. We have outlined the continuing use of the comparative method, and a similar picture may be sketched of the anthropological approach. Since the time of Franz Boas (editor of the *Journal of American Folklore* from 1908 to 1923), many American anthropologists with a special interest in folklore have been intent on documenting the traditions of a people well enough to be able to see the whole culture reflected in its mythology and to explain every nuance of the mythology with reference to the total culture. This "whole-culture" approach requires not only that collectors assemble texts in order to analyze their internal variations, but also that they give full attention to contexts, especially to the various functions of oral tradition in culture and personality.

A leading proponent of the anthropological approach to folklore is William Bascom of the University of California at Berkeley. In "Four Functions of Folklore," *Journal of American Folklore,* 67 (1954), 333–349, Bascom demonstrated how folklore fills particular functions in various cultures: it may simply be a mirror of culture; it may validate aspects of culture; it is a means of education; and it works to maintain conformity to accepted patterns of behavior.

Bascom's 1965 American Folklore Society presidential address, "Folklore, Verbal Art, and Culture," *Journal of American Folklore,* 86 (1973), 374–381, clarifies and defends his much-debated term "verbal art," which he proposed in his article for the *Standard Dictionary of Folklore Mythology and Legend* (New York: Funk & Wagnalls, 1949–1950). Bascom's book *Ifa Divination* (Bloomington: Indiana University Press, 1965) [BF1179/I4/B3] applies the anthropological method to a West African complex of beliefs, customs, and folk narrative.

American anthropological folklorists have been especially active in studies of oral narratives; among major contributors have been Melville J. Herskovits and Frances S. Herskovits in Africa, Katharine Luomala in the South Pacific, Melville Jacobs among Northwest Indian tribes, and Daniel J. Crowley in the West Indies. John Greenway offers a highly personal and often dissenting anthropological view in works such as *Literature among the Primitives* (Hatboro, Pa.: Folklore Associates, 1964) [PN921/G7] and *The Primitive Reader* (Hatboro, Pa.: Folklore Associates, 1965) [GR25/G7].

A group of scholars who have backgrounds in the social sciences rather than exclusively in literary folklore studies continues to advance the anthropological (or, perhaps, "ethnological") approach. The "Culture and Folklore" issue of the *Journal of the Folklore Institute,* edited by Jerome Mintz, 2 (1965), 3–100, offers an overview of the goals of this approach along with six specific studies by various hands. Roger D. Abrahams's *Deep Down in the Jungle; Negro Narrative Folklore from the Streets of Philadelphia* (1964; rev. ed. Chicago: Aldine Press, 1970) [GR103/A2 1970] is an outstanding book-length example.

Psychoanalytic interpretations of folklore, which are ignored or rejected by many folklorists, have nevertheless retained forceful supporters up to the present. Alan Dundes has urged folklorists to pay more heed to the theories of such Freudians as Ernest Jones, who in his lecture "Psychoanalysis and Folklore," delivered before the English Folklore Society in 1928, presented an array of sample interpretations that may be extended considerably with reference to further works by Jones, Erich Fromm, Géza Róheim and others. Pursuing such an approach himself, Dundes has given several folk traditions intriguing Freudian readings that include seeing George

Washington ("The Father of His Country") as an Oedipal figure who symbolically castrated his father by chopping down his cherry tree, retains sexual significance in the widespread identifications of places where he had *slept,* and who has had a phallic monument "erected" to him in the nation's capital.

An important Freudian-oriented study is Gershon Legman's *The Rationale of the Dirty Joke: An Analysis of Sexual Humor,* first series (New York: Grove Press, 1968) [PN6231/S54/L4], which is organized as a simultaneous classification and interpretation. In a valuable in-depth survey, "The Sociopsychological Analysis of Folktales," *Current Anthropology,* 4 (1963), 235–295, J. L. Fischer gathers an extensive bibliography and discusses approaches that may combine anthropological, sociological, and psychological theories and methods. These sorts of studies all have the general objectives, Fischer summarizes, "to discover to what extent and in what way the form and content of tales coming from a given society are related to features of the personality of the bearers of these tales and to features of the social system of these bearers."

Since the first English translation in 1958 of Russian folklorist Vladimir Propp's *The Morphology of the Folktale* (1928) and Alan Dundes's article "From Etic to Emic Units in the Structural Study of Folktales," *Journal of American Folklore,* 75 (1962), 95–105, the structural approach to folklore has become a major trend in American research. This development parallels, as Dundes points out, the movement from prescriptive to descriptive methods in linguistics, which shifted emphasis from diachronic studies (those conceived historically) to synchronic studies (those that disregard historical changes and focus instead on the inner makeup of the material itself).

Structuralism, now a strong movement in European studies as well as those done in the United States, has produced a voluminous literature, and it has spread from folktales to most genres of verbal folklore and to some behavioral and material aspects of folk tradition. (Structural studies are cited according to genres of folklore in the appropriate sections of Chapter 2.) Although this approach may seem directly opposed to the anthropological concern for culturally determined meanings and functions of folklore, its followers promise to eventually show the linkings of the inner patterns found in folk materials to the stereotyped aspects of the broader culture. In this regard, the widely read studies of Claude Lévi-Strauss have been influential.

Choosing an individual approach to folklore study is perhaps not as important to the beginning student-researcher as is learning to make use of whatever theoretical frameworks may provide convincing interpretations and meaningful insights. Or, as D. K. Wilgus has written about what he calls the "rationalistic approach" to folksong studies, "I have yet to find an approach to folksong from which I have not learned something; I have yet to find one whose dominance is not dangerous."

In whatever manner they have approached their studies, one of the most persistent and vexing problems for folklorists has been the definition of the term "folklore" itself, which thus far has eluded them completely. Attempts at definition have ranged from classified lists of folk materials (the strategy of definition by example), to metaphorical statements (the "spirit" of folk tradition), to carefully qualified generalizations (Aristotelian definitions). But all such formulations seem to leave some loose ends dangling, and certainly many folklorists are not satisfied with them.

The frustration in defining "folklore" was illustrated by the decision of the editors of the *Standard Dictionary of Folklore, Mythology, and Legend* in 1959 to have twenty-one contributors each compose a definition of this term. These statements have been reviewed, rejected, revised, and sometimes restored by many different commentators, some of whom point to a "certain core of materials" that most folklorists will agree belong to their field of study; they recognize the basic criteria of oral tradition, variation, anonymity, repetitive form, and ingroup transmission.

Arriving at a definition is complicated by a factor perhaps peculiar to folklore among academic disciplines. There are such powerful, popularized, sentimental, and even pejorative connotations of the term "folklore" in ordinary usage that some scholars have proposed using an alternative label such as "hominology."

The most impressive current movement toward establishing a definition draws its strength from anthropological, behavioral, and rhetorical concepts that recognize folklore (as Roger D. Abrahams puts it) as being that part of any culture that tends to balance traditional stability against dynamic change. The genres of folklore (as Dan Ben-Amos puts it) may best be thought of not in terms of literary types and subtypes, but rather as part of a complex unwritten folkloric system in which every element has its distinct thematic and behavioral attributes in specific contexts. (Dorson has suggested calling this a "contextual" approach.) The broad objective of folklore study, according to Paulo de Carvalho-Neto, is "to discover the rules governing the formation, organization, and metamorphosis of these cultural acts for the benefit of mankind." This is surely an inspiring and worthwhile enterprise, one that need not wait for the writing of a final acceptable definition of folklore. In the meantime, folklorists may expect to continue to operate on the basis of the pragmatic idea overheard at an American Folklore Society conference: "Folklore is what folklorists study."

PROGNOSIS FOR THE FUTURE

Some 130 years after the term "folklore" was coined and the study thus given its putative start, the field seems to be in a healthy state of growth and development. Folklore is well established in colleges and universities, and new folklorists turned out by graduate programs are enlarging the field and its theoretical base steadily through their teaching and writing. There are many outlets now for the publication of research, and the quality of publications as well as papers read at scholarly conferences has improved. One of the healthiest aspects of folkloristics is that the field has been in a constant state of some turmoil and debate (generally conducted in a dignified manner), as folklorists have struggled to work out conceptual and theoretical difficulties in defining and organizing their somewhat amorphous field of inquiry. If anything, this turmoil will increase.

For the immediate future, however, we may expect strong efforts to complete unfinished business: indexes, classifications, editions of texts, encyclopedias, handbooks, folklife atlases, museum treatments of folk traditions, and the like. Also, archival methods need more standardization, and retrieval systems must be further updated if any degree of completeness in reviewing the recorded data on a given folklore subject is to be achieved. Some existing reference works, including the *Motif-Index,* are already in the process of revision; other indexes—those for legends, jokes, ballads, and narrative folksongs, for example—are at least under discussion or have samples in print.

International cooperation in folklore studies will undoubtedly continue and grow. Journals such as *Fabula, Proverbium,* and *Ethnomusicology* have already reached across national boundaries for studies in individual categories of folklore, and we should see more such efforts. Multinational folklore conferences, such as the five-year cycle of meetings of the International Society for Folk-Narrative Research, point the way for other such cooperation. Translations, annotated text editions, foreign exchanges of lecturers and researchers, survey articles on folklore research in other countries, and the publishing of French, German, or English summaries of scholarly articles in journals printed in minor languages are all on the increase and will facilitate better international research. A recent large-scale effort is the Smithsonian/American Folklore Society project for the United States bicentennial celebration, which is bringing together performing groups and other folklore "presenters" from the American immigrant community and from the parent traditions abroad.

All the recent theoretical approaches to folklore are flourishing, particularly the anthropological whole-culture approach, structural analysis, the study of folklife and popular culture, the investigation of modern and urban folklore, and the behavioral or contextual approach. Yet another new concept—"applied folklore"—is still too new to be assessed, but it offers the possibility of going beyond analyzing folklore to actually putting the results of research to work improving people's lives. For example, public health officials and social workers might be made more effective and welcome among groups if they better understood the traditional taboos, beliefs, and medical lore of the people they work with and if they knew how to integrate these traditions with their own scientific training.

The folklorists of today and tomorrow must be willing to take a close hard look at past assumptions and theories in the field and then adopt a broad eclectic approach to research that will draw on the best applicable features of folkloristics and related disciplines. Speaking only about "New Directions for the Study of American Folklore" in 1969, I sketched the following portrait of future folklorists, which need not yet be revised (nor has it been achieved) and which sums things up for the field as a whole:

The future student of the American folk and their lore will have to collect and handle this data like a traditional folklorist, but he will also have to penetrate into its human dynamics like a sociologist, read the language of texts like a psycholinguist, learn to sense implied meanings like an unselfconscious native informant, explicate style and structure like a New Critic, and explore contexts like a cultural anthropologist. A truly comprehensive approach—which I see emerging now in current American folklore research—requires considering folklore simultaneously as a mirror of culture, a projective screen for personality, a response to individual needs and desires, and an artistic expression with its own structures and aesthetics. The study of American folklore should, in short, reveal how individuals project and reflect upon and even modify the ethos of their own culture by means of that unofficial, traditional, and ever-varying part of culture which we loosely call "folklore." (*Folklore*, 82 [1971], 35)

CHAPTER TWO
Reference Guide

❧ ❧ ❧ You cannot become a folklorist simply by reading books and articles, nor can you become one without referring at all to the published record of collections and studies done by others. This chapter, therefore, although not a substitute for the professional training and the fieldwork, archiving, and analysis experience of a seasoned folklorist, rests on the assumption that a student who is directed to reliable publications (and, in addition, is guided by a knowledgeable teacher) is capable of doing worthwhile research in this field without necessarily becoming a fully trained folklorist first. The most important factor here is "reliable publications"; you must read folklore, not fakelore; serious and scholarly research, not romantic ravings about the good old pioneer days or the like.

If only to save an enormous amount of time and energy, the student researcher is well advised to work his or her way into folklore scholarship via the available reference works rather than by just browsing through the library stacks or poking in the card catalogue under subject headings. Browsing and poking around do have their rewards, but getting research finished and papers written are not usually among them. If you have a job to do, you should go about it using the best tools and materials available.

As stated in the first chapter, this guide is disproportionately heavy on works written in English, but care was taken to include in each category the basic sources that lead on to fuller coverage and to the important subareas in each field. Because a number of works apply to more than one category, cross-references have been supplied to indicate the major topic under which such works are discussed; also, the index may be used to locate authors' works concerning a particular approach.

The following sections are arranged from general to specific, progressing from bibliographies and periodical series through folklore surveys, theories, genres, and works of analysis. Each subsection is similarly organized, insofar as possible. Before students begin to look up specific works, it might be useful for them to skim through the whole chapter.

One warning about the Library of Congress number cited for each book: not every library employs exactly the official LC numbers assigned in Washington, and some even use the Dewey Decimal classifications. Thus, if a book is not found shelved at the number shown here, be sure to check the card catalogue of your own library or ask a librarian for assistance. The system for storing reference works and periodicals (both recent and bound issues) varies somewhat from library to library, and this too must be ascertained in each individual library.

BIBLIOGRAPHIES AND REFERENCE WORKS

For the years 1955 through 1962 a well-organized international bibliography of folklore publications was prepared annually for the

American Folklore Society (AFS) and published each following year in the *Journal of American Folklore* "Supplement"; libraries generally (unfortunately, not always) bind this paperbound set of reports and data together with the year's issues of this important quarterly. The last AFS annual bibliography, for 1963, appeared in volume 2 (1964) of the society's new periodical, *Abstracts of Folklore Studies*. *Abstracts* continued through 1975 when it was discontinued; it has been a valuable source of information on new publications, although its selective and often out-of-date summaries of published research were no substitute for a timely comprehensive bibliography.

Fortunately, at about the same time that the AFS annual bibliography disappeared, the folklore section of the huge Modern Language Association (MLA) annual bibliography, previously limited to folklore studies with a literary orientation, was being expanded. Since 1970 this committee-produced effort has come to fill the gap left by the demise of the AFS product; it may be found in the annual bibliography numbers of the society's journal *PMLA*. An important folklore bibliography was included annually from 1937 to 1973 in *Southern Folklore Quarterly*.

Charles Haywood's *A Bibliography of North American Folklore and Folksong* (New York: Greenberg, 1951) [GR101Z/H38] was an ambitious project to fill the great need for a bibliography, and it does indeed bring together hundreds of references, including a great many to American Indian materials ignored in most other folklore bibliographies. It is thoroughly indexed by types, regions, and authors, but its shortcoming is simply that there are great unsuspected gaps and errors in the work as well as many nonfolkloric items; thus users can never be absolutely sure that they have not missed some important works in American folklore. Worse, sometimes the references that Haywood cites simply cannot be found because some of his data (page, volume, year, etc.) are either incomplete or incorrect. Unfortunately, the two-volume paperback reprint (New York: Dover Books, 1961) corrected none of these flaws. Of course, do consult Haywood, but handle with care and search with ingenuity.

Several special survey articles with bibliographies on foreign folklore research were named in the Introduction, and sections of the important but erratically appearing series *Internationale Volkskundliche*

Bibliographie (1917 f.) [Z5982/V92] may be found in some libraries. Few, if any, American libraries possess all the various predecessors and followers of this series, one whole version of which was titled *Bibliographie internationale des arts et traditions populaires*. Ideally, some day, it should be reissued in a standardized format.

Another general bibliography that will be of interest to some students is Ralph Steele Boggs's *Bibliography of Latin American Folklore* (New York: H. W. Wilson, 1940) [GR114Z/B6]. A good bibliographic guide on any particular folklore topic can usually be found in a recent and well-documented book or article on that same topic, such as Horace Beck's *Folklore and the Sea* (Middletown, Conn.: Wesleyan University Press, 1973) [GR910/B37], or Alan Dundes's "On the Structure of the Proverb," *Proverbium*, 25 (1975), 961–973. Bibliographies in textbooks (cited below) may be very useful, but inevitably they are somewhat behind the times.

For a concise summary that is usually helpful and frequently quite authoritative on a multitude of topics, consult the *Standard Dictionary of Folklore, Mythology, and Legend*, 2 vols., edited by Maria Leach and Jerome Fried (New York: Funk & Wagnalls, 1949–1950) [GR35/F8]. Some articles gathered here are detailed, definitive, introductory statements, among them George Herzog's "Song: Folk Song and the Music of Folk Song" and Gertrude P. Kurath's "Dance: Folk and Primitive." Other articles, however, are quite banal and useless, and some major subjects in folklore are not treated at all. The *Standard Dictionary* is best remembered among folklorists for its twenty-one separate definitions of folklore—some directly opposed to others—each written by an individual contributor. Since virtually every library with any pretentions to a folklore collection has the work (a somewhat revised one-volume edition was issued in 1972), and since one never knows when something good may be found in it, folklore researchers starting out with a subject may wish to see what may be lurking in this book, either to guide or misguide them. The contributers' initials and capsule biographies help to give some idea of the reliability of the entries.

A reference work-in-progress with great potential usefulness to folklore studies is the *International Dictionary of Regional European Ethnology and Folklore* (Copenhagen: Rosenkilde and Bagger), which was planned for at least twelve volumes and received support from UNESCO. The two volumes published thus far differ somewhat on their use of English-language citations (though English remains the language for definitions). They are A. Hultkrantz's *General Ethnological Concepts* (1960) and L. Bødker's *Folk-Literature (Germanic)* (1965) [GN307/I5.]

An excellent introduction to the whole range of cultural information that folklorists may concern themselves with, plus a system for classification and tips on collecting, is Séan Ó Súilleabháin's highly inclusive *A Handbook of Irish Folklore* (Dublin, 1942; rpt. Hatboro, Pa.: Folklore Associates, 1963) [GR146/061963]. Since the enormous Irish program of folklore collecting and research was modeled on the longstanding Scandinavian one (particularly the Swedish), this handbook may be taken as a veritable summation of the field of folklore as worked out by some leading European scholars.

Ultimately, the art, craft, or possibly science of folklore *collecting* may perhaps be learned only from experience, and some people never master it at all. It is instructive to encounter such genial souls among fieldworkers as the great Nova Scotia collector W. Roy Mackenzie who described in *The Quest of the Ballad* (Princeton, N.J.: Princeton University Press, 1919) [PR9180/M3] "a few of my successive adventures with the ancient singers of ballads whose society I have eagerly courted during my summer vacations." An especially delightful and practical set of collecting experiences is given by the pioneer American fieldworker John A. Lomax in his *Adventures of a Ballad Hunter* (New York: Macmillan, 1947) [ML429/L68A3]. Lomax wrote of his cowboy singers, "Not one song did I ever get from them except through the influence of generous amounts of whiskey, raw and straight from the bottle or jug."

Folklore collecting techniques and some revealing field anecdotes are presented in the introduction to Richard Dorson's anthology *Buying the Wind* (described under "Folklore Genres," below). A full theoretical and practical treatment of folklore fieldwork was published as volume 52 of the *Memoirs of the American Folklore Society* by its then secretary-treasurer, Kenneth S. Goldstein, as *A Guide for Field Workers in Folklore* (Hatboro, Pa.: American Folklore Society, 1964) [GR1/A5 vol. 52]. A number of collector's guides for individual states have since been published to bring Goldstein's kind of approach down to the individual region; chief among these are the following: MacEdward Leach and Henry

Glassie, *A Guide for Collectors of Oral Traditions and Folk Cultural Material in Pennsylvania* (Harrisburg: Pennsylvania Historical and Museum Commission, 1968); George G. Carey, *Maryland Folklore and Folklife* (Cambridge, Md.: Tidewater Publishers, 1970) [GR110/M3C3]; Jan Harold Brunvand, *A Guide for Collectors of Folklore in Utah* (Salt Lake City: University of Utah Press, 1971) [GR110/U8B78]; and Edward D. Ives, "A Manual for Field Workers," *Northeast Folklore*, 15 (1974).

A convenient list of addresses of the actual depositories of folklore data may be found in Peter Aceves and Magnús Einarsson-Mullarký, *Folklore Archives of the World* (Bloomington, Ind.: *Folklore Forum*, Bibliographic and Special Series, no. 1, 1968).

JOURNALS AND SERIES

There are literally hundreds of periodical series, past and present, devoted to folklore studies and scores of other journals that occasionally publish research in folklore or closely related fields. We mention here only the major ones in English. A list of important foreign journals can be found in Alan Dundes's *The Study of Folklore* (pp. 478–481) described in the next section.

American scholarly journals in folklore are not interested exclusively in one state, region, or even solely in United States material. What most of these journals share in common is simply that they are quarterly publications with folklore society sponsorship and that they are open to contributions of merit concerning any aspect of folklore scholarship. Those journals that do feature some particular emphasis are noted below.

The *Journal of American Folklore* (JAF, 1888 f.) is the oldest, most prestigious, and probably the most internationally inclined periodical of its kind in the United States. As the official organ of the American Folklore Society it tends to attract the cream of the research in essay form by its members, most of whom also subscribe to the society's other quarterly, *Abstracts of Folklore Studies* (1963 f.). An analytical index to *JAF* through volume 70 was published in 1957.

The oldest continuous regional folklore journal in the United States is the *Tennessee Folklore Society Bulletin* (TFSB, 1934 f.);

this journal, although still in its original modest mimeographed format, has held to a consistently high standard of studies, mainly Tennessean or at least regional. A useful survey of folklore serials in the United States prepared by William J. Griffin was published in *TFSB*, 25 (1959), 91–96. Second place for longevity goes to *Southern Folklore Quarterly* (*SFQ*, 1937 f.), published by the South Atlantic Modern Language Association. *SFQ* included until 1973 an annual bibliography with special emphasis on Latin American folklore, and over the years it has been the one journal of its kind to regularly include studies of folklore in relation to literature.

Predating these two, as an annual collection of essays rather than a quarterly journal, is *Publications of the Texas Folklore Society* (*PTFS*, 1924 f.). Here, for once, there has been a strong emphasis on material from the state of the sponsoring folklore society. A sometimes confusing aspect of *PTFS* is that each annual volume bears a snappy title (*And Horns on the Frogs, The Sunny Slopes of Long Ago*, etc.) as well as its serial numbering in the general series. An analytical index of volumes 1 through 36 was published in 1973.

Two state folklore journals that began publication in 1942 eventually developed into new and less regional formats. *Hoosier Folklore Bulletin* (*HFB*) has undergone the most radical metamorphosis, as mentioned in Chapter 1. In 1946 it was replaced by *Hoosier Folklore* (*HF*); then in 1951 *HF* in turn gave way to *Midwest Folklore* (*MF*), which itself ceased publication with volume 13 (1963), only to be replaced by the ongoing *Journal of the* [Indiana University] *Folklore Institute* (*JFI*, 1964 f.). The gap in folklore publication from the state of Indiana was filled by a new semiannual journal *Indiana Folklore* (*IF*, 1968 f.). The second journal to start in 1942 was *California Folklore Quarterly* (*CFQ*), which changed only its name (retaining the volume numbering) and has been known as *Western Folklore* (*WF*) since 1947; a twenty-five year index to *CFQ*/*WF* was published in 1966.

The *New York Folklore Quarterly* (*NYFQ*) continued with the same title and format from 1945 to 1975; folklore in education is one of its specialties. It has been replaced with a journal called *New York Folklore* (*NYF*). Other continuing state and regional folklore quarterlies are *New Mexico Folklore Record* (*NMFR*, 1946 f.),

Kentucky Folklore Record (KFR, 1955 f.), *Keystone Folklore Quarterly* (KFQ, 1956 f., now simply *Keystone Folklore*), *North Carolina Folklore Journal* (NCFJ, 1954 f., formerly *North Carolina Folklore*), *Mississippi Folklore Register* (MFR, 1967 f.), and *Mid-South Folklore* (MSF, 1973 f.). The journal *Northeast Folklore* (NEF, 1958 f.), first a quarterly, has appeared instead as an annual since 1962. *Northwest Folklore* (NWF, 1965 f.), a semiannual publication, ceased publication with volume 4 in 1968. Another recent regional folklore journal is titled *AFFword* (1971 f.), with reference to its sponsoring organization, the Arizona Friends of Folklore. So far this publishing effort has not only survived but also sustained the unequaled feat of producing for sale each year a recording of authentic regional folk music.

A defunct series of considerable importance is the *Folklore and Folk Music Archivist* (FFMA) distributed by the Indiana University Archive of Traditional Music from 1958 to 1968 (10 volumes, 35 individual issues). The last issue of *FFMA* (vol. 10, no. 3, Spring 1968) contained a full cumulative index of its contents, which consisted of mostly useful articles on folklore archives and archiving techniques.

In 1968, graduate students at Indiana University began a new journal, *Folklore Forum* (FF), which soon received support from other campuses and expanded in size from its original half-dozen sheets (though it is still only mimeographed and stapled). The *Forum* challenged academic decorum and precedent by such means as criticizing the practices of other folklore journals, taking editorial stands, awarding monetary prizes for important new writings, and soliciting special articles on neglected subjects (such as the teaching of folklore). In 1969, folklore students at the University of Texas began the publication of *Folklore Annual*, containing their own scholarly papers. (At this point perhaps it should be mentioned that most folklore journals do have special lower subscription rates for students; see their inside front covers for current information.)

The latest low-budget, special-interest, noninstitutional American folklore journal is *Folklore Feminists Communication* (FFemC, 1973 f.), which appears three times a year with reports and studies relevant to women's interests in regard to folklore and folkloristics.

Among the scores of foreign folklore journals, many American students may want to consult mainly *Folklore* (1878 f.), the quarterly of the English Folklore Society, which has been publishing ten years longer than its American counterpart. Two foreign journals, one from Germany and the other from Finland, specialize in studies of a particular folklore genre, and they include frequent articles in English along with other major modern languages. These are *Fabula: Journal of Folktale Studies* (1959 f.) and *Proverbium* (1965 f.), which began its first volume with a useful discussion by Archer Taylor, "The Study of Proverbs."

Nonfolklore journals of some interest to folklorists include *American Speech* (*AS*, 1925 f.), *Names* (1953 f.), and the *Journal of Popular Culture* (*JPC*, 1967 f.). Of course, many of the literary and general humanistic or social science research quarterlies also publish articles on folklore from time to time; these may be found by means of bibliographies in *Abstracts of Folklore Studies* or sometimes just through serendipitous browsing in libraries.

Finally, it is necessary to mention several continuing publication series that are not periodicals proper. In some libraries, they may be catalogued and shelved as a group rather than according to their individual titles and subject matter. (Elsewhere in this guide these are treated as independent books.) The *Folklore Fellows Communications* (*FFC*) is one of the oldest of these series, having begun in 1910 mainly as an outlet for substantial contributions to the historic-geographic analysis of folktales. Published in Helsinki, Finland, and edited by an international committee, typical *FFC* issues (each one separately numbered but in a fixed format) have included type indexes and catalogues, studies of individual tale types, theoretical essays, collections of related shorter studies, and some research findings on genres such as games, ballads, and gestures. The language of *FFC* publication is German or (most often nowadays) English.

The American Folklore Society sponsors two monograph series in which numerous important catalogues, collections, and studies have been published; these are the "Memoir Series" and the "Bibliographical and Special Series." (Apparently imitating the AFS, *Folklore Forum* recently introduced a "Bibliographic and Special Series.") Three American universities sponsor occasional publications in special "Folklore Series"; these are Indiana University, the University of California, and recently the University of Pennsylvania.

FOLKLORE HISTORIES, SURVEYS, AND TEXTBOOKS

Essential to a good understanding of theories and methods in any academic field is a solid grasp of the historical antecedents and underlying principles of the field. Unfortunately, the history of folklore studies has been only skimpily compiled and written thus far, and most of the important longer studies are not available in English. The one general history of European folklore scholarship, for example, is in Italian: Giuseppe Cocchiara's *Storia del folklore in Europa*, 2d ed. (Torino: Einaudi, 1952) [GR135/C6]. For the Danish survey "The History of Folklore Research in Central and Northern Europe" by Inger M. Boberg (*Folkemindeforskningens Historie i Mellem— og Nordeuropa*; Copenhagen: Danmarks Folkeminder, no. 60, 1953) [GR210/D2 no. 60], there is an English summary.

For biographies of northern European pioneers in folklore study, one may consult Dag Strömbäck, ed., *Leading Folklorists of the North* (Oslo: Scandinavian University Books, 1971) [GR50/B5]; and for reference to perhaps the leading Scandinavian group of folklorists in their earliest period of growth, see Jouko Hautala, *Finnish Folklore Research, 1828–1919* (Helsinki: Societas Scientiarum Fennica, 1969) [GR200/H35].

More biographies and critical evaluations of the works of major folklorists are needed to help complete the groundwork for better historic studies of the whole field. Although flawed by hazy notions of folklore theory and terminology, two recent biographies of the Grimm brothers are useful: Ruth Michaelis-Jena, *The Brothers Grimm* (New York: Praeger, 1970) [PD64/G7/M5], and M. B. Peppard, *Paths Through the Forest, a Biography of the Brothers Grimm* (New York: Holt, Rinehart and Winston, 1971) [PD64/ G7P4]. Combining, extending, and supplementing his series of historical articles, Richard M. Dorson produced a valuable background study for English and Anglo-American folklore development, *The British Folklorists* (Chicago: University of Chicago Press, 1968) [GR50/D63]. This narrative history is accompanied by two volumes of selections from writings of British folklorists: *Peasant Customs and Savage Myths* (Chicago: University of Chicago Press, 1968) [GR141/D6 1968b].

The history of American folkloristics has been taken up only in journal articles, such as Alan Dundes, "Robert Lee Vance, American Folklore Surveyor of the 1890's," *Western Folklore*, 23 (1964), 27–34; Richard M. Dorson, "Elsie Clews Parsons: Feminist and Folklorist," *AFFword*, 1 (1971), 1–4 (reprinted in *Folklore Feminists Communication*, no. 2 [1974], 4 ff.); and Keith S. Chambers, "The Indefatigable Elsie Clews Parsons—Folklorist," *Western Folklore*, 32 (1973), 180–198. An especially important group of such articles appeared in the "American Folklore Historiography" issue of the *Journal of the Folklore Institute*, 10 (1973), 3–128, edited by Richard A. Reuss.

A history of part of the larger subject is available in the publication of a series of lectures given at the University of California at Los Angeles by Paulo de Carvalho-Neto, *History of Iberoamerican Folklore: Mestizo Cultures,* with a foreword by Wayland D. Hand (Oosterhout, Holland: Anthropological Publications, 1969) [GR114/C3713]. In what might be a likely model for future studies, Carvalho-Neto surveys for each general area of his concern the following topics: precursors, systematizers, researchers, complementary contributions, genres and types, and examples.

Several general surveys of folklore materials and methods were described in Chapter 1; their chief value lies in the overview of the subject that they provide for students; they can help students to organize their research and frame it in the context of the total discipline. In this regard, a work that is basic despite its being outdated and its author sometimes betraying certain quirks is Alexander Haggerty Krappe's *The Science of Folklore* (1930; paperback rpt. New York: W. W. Norton, 1964) [GR65/K7]. Krappe expended much energy attacking the British anthropological school and promoting the emerging Finnish literary approach, and he denied that American folklore existed. However, his erudition and the wide scope of his view over the whole field of folklore keeps the book readable, quotable, and even occasionally teachable by contemporary folklorists.

A wish to "update Krappe" (whether so stated or not) has resulted in at least three attempts at current international survey works, all collaborative volumes and none really quite like the original. A curious work—sketchy in some areas, detailed in others—is J. Russell Reaver and George W. Boswell's *Fundamentals of Folk Literature*

(Oosterhout, Holland: Anthropological Publications, 1962) [GR45/B6]. Despite its general title, the work is based largely on examples from one state—Tennessee. The eight chapters on folksong in Reaver/Boswell are the book's best feature; the bibliographies and "projects" for each section tend to be uneven and limited. Too often discussions of genres conclude indecisively with only lists of partly relevant examples or with generalizations on the order of "There is no question that something called folklore does exist and is both interesting and important." Suffering many of the same faults as this work is Kenneth Clarke and Mary Clarke's *Introducing Folklore* (New York: Holt, Rinehart and Winston, 1963) [GR40/C54]. As an overall survey it is somewhat disorganized and often sketchy; however, it has a valuable section entitled "The Student Folklorist" as well as worthwhile (though rather irrelevant) sections on the authors' own specialties—West African folktales and folk idiom in the writings of the Cumberland Mountains regional author Jesse Stuart. A sample of the Clarkes' frequently confusing style is this introduction to the problem of defining folklore: "Another note about the substance of the study of folklore is actually many definitions, most of which are so vague as to be mere impressions." Folklore, in their view, "consists of all lore (knowledge, wisdom, action) transmitted by tradition."

Unlike the two books just described, the latest and by far most successful survey includes material and behavioral materials as well as the more commonly studied verbal lore, as is reflected in its title, *Folklore and Folklife: An Introduction* (Chicago: University of Chicago Press, 1972) [GR65/D57]. The book is edited by Richard M. Dorson, who contributes a good introduction on concepts of folklore plus a chapter on using printed sources, and contains solid discussions on most major folk genres by authorities of international renown, each of whom also compiled a selective annotated bibliography. A separate section deals with "The Methods of Folklife Study," and the whole work is well indexed and suitably illustrated with both photographs and drawings. Only the disparate styles of the various contributors tend to detract from the readability of the book as a general survey; however, since most readers will consult the chapters separately for reference to individual topics, this is not really a serious problem. The concise discussions of such topics as folk religion, costume, and cookery are unequaled by anything else available in English, and the chapters on fieldwork, archiving, atlases, and folk museums are the most current English surveys of these matters.

An older, rather obscure but still useful survey of folklore research in a social science framework may be found in the essay by E. J. Lindgren, "The Collection and Analysis of Folklore " (pp. 328–378), in F. C. Bartlett, ed., *The Study of Society* (London: Routledge & Kegan Paul, 1939) [HM24/B35]. A recent selection of readings in cultural anthropology by an anthropologically oriented folklorist would broaden any literary folklorist's base of operations considerably; in this regard see the extensive bibliographic notes in Alan Dundes, ed., *Every Man His Way* (Englewood Cliffs, N.J.: Prentice-Hall, 1968) [GN325/D8]; of specific interest to folklorists in this volume is Dundes's own previously unpublished essay, "The Number Three in American Culture" (pp. 401–424).

Collections of essays by prominent folklorists, garnered from the back issues of scholarly journals, serve as useful surveys of the field and its diverse practitioners. Dundes's *The Study of Folklore* (Englewood Cliffs, N.J.: Prentice-Hall, 1965) [GR45/D8] is particularly important as it includes not only well-known American essays such as William Bascom's "Four Functions of Folklore" and Archer Taylor's "Folklore and the Student of Literature," but also less accessible pieces such as Stith Thompson's "The Star Husband Tale" and an original translation of Axel Olrik's "Epic Laws of Folk Narrative." Dundes arranged his selections under the headings "What is Folklore?" "The Search for Origins," "Form in Folklore," "The Transmission of Folklore," "The Functions of Folklore," and "Selected Studies." The coverage is wide, and choices of articles are sound; the editor's comments and footnotes ably weld the anthology into a coherent whole.

A collection of thirteen essays by Louise Pound deals mainly with the regional material indicated by its title: *Nebraska Folklore* (Lincoln: University of Nebraska Press, 1959) [GR110/N2/P6]. Miss Pound was a literary and linguistic scholar of distinction, the first woman elected president of the Modern Language Society, as well as a folklorist. Three more general essays appended to the book, especially "The Scholarly Study of Folklore," are reliable and recom-. mended. The latest such compilation of an American folklorist's writings for periodicals is Richard M. Dorson's *Folklore: Selected*

Essays (Bloomington: Indiana University Press, 1972) [GR71/ D67]. This is a set of eleven essays on subjects ranging from folklore theory, methodology, and history to examinations of oral style, legend tradition, tall tales, and the academic future of folklore. Written in Dorson's characteristically good-humored and anecdotal style, the book is much more readable than the standardized format of such harvests might at first suggest. The subject index (a feature lacking in the Dundes and Pound books) is a useful addition and did not appear in the original publications of the essays.

National folklore survey volumes are generally published only in the language of their nations; an important exception is Y. M. Sokolov's *Russian Folklore* (New York: Macmillan, 1950) [GR190/ S624], which is valuable not only as a summary of materials and research but perhaps more importantly as a source of information (especially evident in different editions of the work) about political reinterpretations of folklore by the Soviets. An interesting view by a leading Norwegian scholar of the folklore from Europe that became assimilated into American culture is Reidar Christiansen's work *European Folklore in America,* published as number 12 of the series *Studia Norvegica* (Oslo, 1962) [GR220/S85].

Many books already described and some yet to be named in later sections of this chapter have been either published specifically as textbooks or adopted for such use; there remain to be mentioned only three books that are primarily American college folklore texts. Richard M. Dorson's *American Folklore* (Chicago: University of Chicago Press, 1959) [GR105/D65] was treated in Chapter 1 as an important landmark of synthesis and interpretation that set forth the major oral traditions of the United States in a sound historical context. The book has survived well as a text and reference work, although the passage of time has inevitably made its bibliographic notes incomplete and such references as "GI Joe," "Betty Coed," and perhaps even "the Negro" dated. Dorson was also one of the twenty-six American folklore scholars to contribute to Tristram Potter Coffin's compilation *Our Living Traditions: An Introduction to American Folklore* (New York: Basic Books, 1968) [GR105/C6]. Originally presented as a series of broadcasts for Voice of America, the various essays thereby acquired (depending upon the skills of contributors) a certain clear readability or an unfortunate oversimplified generality. Some topics seldom treated in general essays are surveyed here—lyric folksongs, labor lore, folklore and the mass media; the five essays in the section "Folklore as a Field for Study" were written by major scholars, most of the works up to a fairly high standard. Unfortunately, the book has no bibliography, except for casual references in the essays themselves.

The latest American folklore textbook—the only one to be organized around genres since Levette Davidson's of 1951 (see Chapter 1) —is *The Study of American Folklore: An Introduction* (New York: W. W. Norton, 1968) [GR105/B7] by the author of this guide, Jan Harold Brunvand. Abandoning humility, I shall simply quote my own words to describe the textbook:

> [It has] a title as audacious as Child's *The English and Scottish Popular Ballads.* The book is notable for what it gets away with: a formal definition of folklore, a detailed classification of genres, and numerous examples of sub-categories . . . chapters on folklife subjects, along with sample studies of customary and material folklore . . . more currently viable folklore than archaic tradition, . . . samples of antisocial and obscene folklore. (*Folklore*, 82 [1971], 29)

Teachers and students have commended the book's bibliographies and the straightforward, if somewhat prosaic, explication of genres. Most often they criticize its weakness on subtleties of theory and its sometimes arbitrary order of subjects which separates custom from belief, music from song lyrics, game rhymes from games, and the like. Be that as it may, beginning researchers in most areas of American folklore should find the concise discussions of genres and the detailed bibliographic notes in *The Study of American Folklore* instructive.

THEORIES OF FOLKLORE

In order to gain a balanced awareness of theory in folklore research—especially of modern theories—students must turn more to essays in recent periodicals than to books. The bibliographies and footnotes in these articles can lead them to older theoretical works or to more elaborated writings on theory in books. Since present folklore studies, particularly in the United States, are in the midst of a major upheaval with regard to theory, many of the works described here take the form of debates or challenges to past concepts and procedures. The beginning reader of theoretical folkloristic works, therefore, must be prepared, now more than ever, to find folklorists disagreeing with each other in print; this is particularly true of important folklorists who are cited repeatedly in this section.

Richard M. Dorson offers a convenient summary of "Current Folklore Theories" with an extensive bibliography in *Current Anthropology*, 4 (1963), 93–112. He identifies five basic trends or schools: comparative, national, anthropological, psychoanalytical, and structural. A longer list may be found in his introduction to *Folklore and Folklife: An Introduction*, described in the previous section. Here, Dorson distinguishes "historical-geographical" theory from "historical-reconstructional"; substitutes "functional" for the anthropological label and "hemispheric" for the national one; and adds to his list of theories "ideological," "oral-formulaic," "cross cultural," "folk-cultural," "mass-cultural," and "contextual." Taken together, these two pieces serve as an excellent general introduction to the fundamental theoretical stances taken by folklorists.

There are already in print many writings attesting to the ferment now working in modern American folklore scholarship. Most of these works have originated in the numerous and lively debates heard at annual conventions of the American Folklore Society or of regional scholarly groups. Students may acquire a good sense of this ongoing debate and further ground themselves in elements of folklore theory by reading through a series of such pieces. The subject most often and most hotly debated (touched on in Chapter 1) is the definition of folklore.

At the 1967 annual meeting of the AFS in Toronto, Canada, Dan Ben-Amos delivered a paper (originally titled "Folklore: The Definitions Game Once Again") that opened with a detailed critique of typical item-oriented, genre-dominated definitions of folklore (whether "enumerative, intuitive, or operational"). He asserted in opposition that "in its cultural context, folklore is not an aggregate of things, but a process—a communicative process, to be exact." Ben-Amos's own definition, growing out of the concept of the "folkloric act" rather than of folklore as a body of "traditional artifacts," was: "Folklore is artistic communication in small groups." This entire essay ("Toward a Definition of Folklore in Context") deserves close reading for the full development of its argument, as well as for the useful footnoted summary of past definitions of folklore. It can be found, along with a group of other groundbreaking essays, in a special issue of the *Journal of American Folklore*: "Toward New Perspectives in Folklore," 84 (1971), which also appeared the same year as number 23 in the AFS Bibliographical and Special Series.

In an unusual step, the *Journal of American Folklore* published a comment by Roger L. Welsch on Ben-Amos's paper even before it had been submitted to a journal. In "A Note on Definitions," *JAF*, 81 (1968), 262–264, Welsch remarked on the "acute frustration," as if "possessed by some definitional demon," that American folklorists seem to suffer from in their repeated efforts to redefine "folklore" in some kind of scientific and logically consistent terms. Observing that by nature linguistic meanings are not historically bound, that language (and definition) is arbitrary and conventional, and that working definitions only need be stated clearly and applied efficiently, Welsch concluded that "there is no need for a new definition or a defense of an old one. In fact, there is no need for *a* definition." Fittingly, on the facing page of the same journal the outgoing editor had added to his own departure message that "[it is now] unnecessary for authors to give him the pleasure of reading any more definitions of folklore."

Roger Welsch's note quickly drew replies from two leading advocates of what Dorson has called the new "contextual" approach to folkloristics. In "Towards a Behavioral Theory of Folklore," *JAF*, 82 (1969), 167–170, Richard Bauman concisely set forth a well-argued support of Ben-Amos's "major reconceptualization of the entire field of folklore." Stressing anew that folklore is not "things" or "materials" but should be considered in terms of "communicative process," Bauman tentatively advocated "the application of a set of parametric dichotomies as a means of defining the realm of folklore communication in such a way that it can be related to other kinds of behavior at the level of each cut." On this basis he suggested that folklore might then be seen as "inter-personal, noncasual, expressive communication" at least from one behavioral-analytical point of view. Welsch's one-sentence response printed after Bauman's statement concluded, "I shall continue to believe that the strength of American Folklore studies lies not in a proposed unanimity of thought but rather in inevitable diversity."

Roger D. Abrahams's answer to Welsch turned to a critique of definitions of folklore in two recent textbooks; see "On Meaning and

Gaming," *JAF*, 82 (1969), 268–270. Scoring the authors for conceiving of folklore in terms of items instead of process and for failing to examine theoretical bases of generalizations, Abrahams claimed that "we need to progress to a method of analysis that will allow us to see lore in all its dimensions, as existing in a specific time and place and yet capable of crossing linguistic, cultural, and historical boundaries." For the reply of one textbook author, see Jan Harold Brunvand, "On Abrahams' Besom," *JAF*, 83 (1970), 81. Mercifully, this series of debates concluded with this atrociously punningly titled squib.

Having now identified some active players and some strategies in the redefinition-reconceptualizing folklore game, the student should go on to further and newer writings in the same vein, of which the following are only a bare sample. Roger D. Abrahams, in his "Introductory Remarks to a Rhetorical Theory of Folklore," *Journal of American Folklore*, 81 (1968), 143–158, looked at the gap between literary and anthropological approaches to folklore study and found in the approach of Kenneth Burke to "situations and strategies" of poetry a new way of coordinating studies of "performance, item and audience" in folklore. Abrahams illustrated such a method cogently with capsule analyses of certain proverbs and riddles in their social and cultural contexts. Dan Ben-Amos put forth his point in "Analytical Categories and Ethnic Genres," *Genre*, 2 (1969), 275–301. Here he summarized the thematic, holistic, archetypal, and functional approaches to defining folklore genres, proposing in place of them a study of thematic and behavioral attributes that seem to belong with a given genre as part of a culture's "grammar of folklore," an approach that was illustrated with examples from Nigeria.

An example of one of the "young Turks" of American folklore taking on a long-held theoretical assumption with characteristic verve and learning is Alan Dundes's attack, "The Devolutionary Premise in Folklore Theory," *Journal of the Folklore Institute*, 6 (1969), 5–19. In an earlier issue of the same journal Dundes published a useful summary, "The American Concept of Folklore," *JFI*, 3 (1966), 226–245, which had originally been written for delivery at a European conference. A recent attack upon established folkloristic terminology and assumptions from the viewpoint of the philosophy and history of scientific method is Kenneth Laine Ketner's

"The Role of Hypotheses in Folkloristics," *Journal of American Folklore*, 86 (1973), 114–130, which was answered by Anne Cohen and Norm Cohen in "A Word on Hypotheses," *JAF*, 87 (1974), 156–160.

The only possible conclusion to the present survey of folklore theory is that there *is* no conclusion. If you look into almost any recent issue of a major folklore journal, you are likely to be plunged back into the center of the ongoing debate over modern theory.

A baker's dozen of influential theoretical essays by a leading Swedish folklorist, translated into English or in German with English summaries, is available in C. W. von Sydow, *Selected Papers on Folklore* (Copenhagen: Rosenkilde and Bagger, 1948) [GR20/S9]. A lasting impression has been made upon modern scholars by, in particular, von Sydow's criticisms of the historic-geographic method, his ideas about genres of oral prose narrative, and his discussion of active and passive carriers of tradition. Even a stronger influence—that of the structural approach—was belatedly felt in Western Europe and the United States from the original works of the Russian folklorist Vladimir Propp, whose *Morphology of the Folktale* (1928) was first published in an English translation only in 1958 and issued in a second corrected edition in 1968 (Austin, Texas: AFS Memoir Series, vol. 9) [GR550/P7613 1968]. Although Propp's schematic reduction of a selected corpus of Russian fairy tales to *one* master outline of elements (called "functions") may seem remote and arbitrary to beginning readers in structural folklore analysis, introductory chapters and bibliographies prepared by Svatava Pirkova-Jakobson and Alan Dundes (both printed in the second edition) deal with some objections to this approach and the possibilities for wider application. The best sources in which to further pursue the structural approach might be two works by Elli Köngäs Maranda and Pierre Maranda, *Structural Models in Folklore and Transformational Essays* (The Hague: Mouton and Co., Approaches to Semiotics, no. 10, 1971) [GR40/M28] and *Structural Analysis of Oral Tradition* (Philadelphia: University of Pennsylvania Press, Publications in Folklore and Folklife, no. 3, 1971) [GR40/M3].

The psychoanalytic approach to folklore has many adherents who are not professional folklorists; very few folklorists seem to be well informed concerning it, although a few do practice and promote it ably. Among the latter is Alan Dundes, whose foreword to Paulo de Carvalho-Neto's *Folklore and Psychoanalysis* (1956; Eng. trans. Coral Gables, Fla.: University of Miami Press, 1972) [GR40/ C38613] is an excellent survey for this subject.

Among the many possible theoretical and methodological applications of folklore study to other scholarly fields, those involving either history or literature are perhaps most commonly recognized. Richard M. Dorson's collected essays, *American Folklore and the Historian* (Chicago: University of Chicago Press, 1971) [GR105/D655], is a good introduction to the application to history, with its discussions of such topics as folklore and fakelore, folklore and American studies, use of printed sources, American historical legends, and folklore in American literature. A rare book-length study (Dorson's notes contain mostly references to essays) concerning folklore and American literature is Daniel Hoffman's *Form and Fable in American Fiction* (New York: Oxford University Press, 1961; corrected paperback ed. New York: Galaxy Books, 1965) [PS377/H6]. Similar to Hoffman's book, with an emphasis on major American authors and basic literary trends but with even less reference to the actual materials of American folklore, is Gene Bluestein's *The Voice of the Folk: Folklore and American Literary Theory* (Amherst: University of Massachusetts Press, 1972) [GR105/B485]. Much more to the point, and an excellent study in its own right, is Ronald L. Baker's *Folklore in the Writings of Rowland E. Robinson* (Bowling Green, Ohio: Bowling Green University Popular Press, 1973) [PS2719/ R68Z6].

To move beyond only American folklore/literary connections, students must turn to general bibliographies and indexes, for although many special studies of folklore can be found in specific authors, works, and periods, there are no broad-scale surveys of importance.

Folklorists have begun to explore the interrelationships between folklore and mass culture, particularly in some issues of the *Journal of Popular Culture,* but also in recent folklore periodicals. An essay on "Popular Culture in the Folklore Course" by Jan Harold Brunvand attempts to place these fields in some workable relationship to each other; the essay is included in Ray B. Browne and Ronald J. Ambrosetti, eds., *Popular Culture and Curricula* (Bowling Green, Ohio: Bowling Green University Popular Press, 1970) [LB15170/

P64], pp. 59–72. One imaginative project involved monitoring one full day of television programming looking for folkloric references. This was analyzed in Tom Burns's "Folklore in the Mass Media: Television," *Folklore Forum*, 2 (1969), 90–106. Alan Dundes has made some interesting observations in "Advertising and Folklore," *New York Folklore Quarterly*, 19 (1963), 143–151. From a theoretical point of view, the mass-cultural approach is intriguing because it tests several of our old traditional concepts of folklore against contemporary situations; from a practical point of view, the folklore/ "poplore" area offers almost limitless, untouched, and ever-changing opportunities for new investigations.

FOLKLORE GENRES

Despite theoretical questions concerning the validity of distinguishing analytical categories of folklore, the student folklorist must nevertheless operate within the traditional scholarly generic terms and groupings, if only to be able to use most folklore archives, bibliographies, and publications. Therefore, although questions are now being raised about the relevance of "types of folklore" to any true understanding of folk communication and process (as the previous section attests), it is a matter of practical convenience to approach many of the basic classifications, editions, and studies of folk materials in the way many of them were first conceived—by genres. Depending upon the completeness of the analyses and background information in such works, even modern anthropologically oriented folklorists may find data in them that are useful in their own research.

State folklore collections that include examples of standard genres classified systematically and discussed comparatively are useful for orienting oneself to a large variety of materials and for directing one's attention to related published sources. A number of such general collections have been published, chief among them the *Frank C. Brown Collection of North Carolina Folklore*, Newman Ivey White, gen. ed., 7 vols. (Durham, N.C.: Duke University Press, 1952–1964) [GR110/N8D8]. English professor and university administrator Frank C. Brown (1870–1943), although a collector of voluminous oral and customary folk materials, did little classification and less analysis of his hoard; it was left for a committee of authorities on the individual genres of folklore to edit and annotate his collection for publication. The result is a set of individual compilations (proverbs, ballads and folksongs, music of the folk ballads and songs, superstitions, etc.), each arranged and analyzed by a specialist with full reference to the bibliographic backgrounds of that type. Except for the lack of much contextual data and the slighting of material folk traditions, the Brown collection is a model work, unparalleled among other states.

A one-volume compendium of various selected folklore types, or folklore from various groups, drawn from a single state's traditions is another familiar kind of publication that is useful for purposes of orientation. Harold W. Thompson's *Body, Boots and Britches* (Philadelphia: Lippincott, 1940) [F120/T55], on New York State, and George Korson's *Pennsylvania Songs and Legends* (Philadelphia: University of Pennsylvania Press, 1949) [ML3551/K85] are older well-documented examples of similar scope. Both books include sections on the Anglo-American heritage, immigrant folklore, occupational groups, tall tales, folksongs, and the like, and both are well annotated. Newer state collections from the West include S. J. Sackett and William E. Koch's *Kansas Folklore* (Lincoln: University of Nebraska Press, 1961) [GR110/K2S3] and Roger L. Welsch's *A Treasury of Nebraska Pioneer Folklore* (Lincoln: University of Nebraska Press, 1966) [GR110/N2W4]. Both depart somewhat from "oral literature" to include such types as folk dances, games, and recipes.

Folklore collections from relatively small and culturally homogeneous districts within states or that overlap state boundaries allow better possibilities for thorough coverage of genres and more meaningful interpretation. A fine example of this approach was made by Emelyn E. Gardner, whose *Folklore from the Schoharie Hills, New York* (Ann Arbor: University of Michigan Press, 1937) [GR110/N7G3] was based on six summers of fieldwork and the collector's solid background in folklore scholarship. Richard Dorson refers to her as a "sterling fieldworker" whose book is "the most skillful American collection of the full range of a folklore within a limited area." Dorson's own *Bloodstoppers and Bearwalkers: Folk Traditions of the Upper Peninsula* (Cambridge, Mass.: Harvard University Press, 1952; paperback rpt. 1972) [GR110/M6D6] is another classic of this kind of study, and it includes examples and discussions of the fascinating mix of native, immigrant, and occupational folklore of this relatively isolated semiwilderness area in northern Michigan. Ambitious anthologies of varied folk materials that attempt to present whole nations at a single gulp are seldom successful in a scholarly sense, although such works have often enjoyed enormous sales as coffee-table books and general library references. The scope of these works is too broad for genuine representativeness, and trade-book publishers can seldom be convinced to publish more than a modicum of notes along with a grab bag of folk texts. In the United States in particular such "treasuries" suffer from an uncritical selection of examples and from limited and romantic concepts of folklore. Even an anthology such as Tristram P. Coffin and Hennig Cohen's *Folklore in America* (Garden City, N.Y.: Doubleday, 1966; paperback rpt. 1970) [GR105/J65], although made up entirely of materials from the *Journal of American Folklore,* wrenches its texts away from the interpretive context of the articles in which they originally appeared and includes some quite inconsequential examples, apparently just to gain ethnic variety and regional balance. A much more successful collection is Richard M. Dorson's *Buying the Wind: Regional Folklore in the United States* (Chicago: University of Chicago Press, 1964) [GR105/D66], which confines itself to only seven folk groups and sets the annotated texts of each group against a review of studies concerning the whole folklife tradition of that group. (The seven groups are Maine down-easters, Pennsylvania Dutchmen, Southern mountaineers, Louisiana Cajuns, Illinois Egyptians, Southwest Mexicans, and Utah Mormons.) A bonus in *Buying the Wind* (the title refers to a Maine sailors' legend) is Dorson's informative introductory essay "Collecting Oral Folklore in the United States."

FOLKSAY

The short, verbal, nonnarrative forms of folklore—dialect, naming, proverbs, riddles, rhymes, and all their subtypes—may be subsumed under the general heading "folksay." Although this term is not universally employed by folklorists for these genres, it leads to no confusion of meaning and does set up a nice parallel with "folktale," "folksong," "folk dance," and the like.

The purely linguistic component of traditional speech patterns is, of course, a subject of primary concern for linguists proper, and folklorists often confine their work in this area to explicating dialect patterns in longer folk texts. A concise introduction to this field of study may be found in Raven I. McDavid, "Linguistic Geography and the Study of Folklore," *New York Folklore Quarterly*, 14 (1958), 242–262. Dictionaries of dialect usages are useful for establishing variant meanings, checking etymologies, finding earliest dates of occurrences, and the like. Two typical such works are Mitford M. Mathews, *A Dictionary of Americanisms on Historical Principles* (Chicago: University of Chicago Press, 1951) [PE2835/D5], and Harold Wentworth and Stuart Berg Flexner, *Dictionary of American Slang* (New York: T. Y. Crowell, 1967) [PE3729/U5W4]. Similar dictionaries from other languages and groups may be found usually in the reference section in the same library category, along with such specialized works as Walter F. McCulloch, *Woods Words: A Comprehensive Dictionary of Loggers' Terms* (Portland: Oregon Historical Society, 1958) [PE3727/L8M3].

Most studies of individual folk expressions have been published as essays in scholarly journals, such as Allen Walker Read's fascinating "The Folklore of O.K.," *American Speech*, 39 (1964), 5–25. After sifting through numerous fanciful interpretations of this most common of traditional sayings, Read concludes that an 1839 reference to "oll korrect" probably predated and spawned all others. Of particular interest to folklorists is Peter Tamony's examination " 'Hootenanny': the Word, Its Content and Continuum," *Western Folklore*, 22 (1963), 165–170. Contrary to popular assumptions, "hootenanny" represents neither a pioneer custom nor term, having been adopted in the early days of the folksong revival by citybilly singers who gathered it from the tradition of such "indefinable words" as "wingding," "thingamagig," and "doodad."

Linguistic geographers have published a great many essays and books dealing with regional dialects, but only two folkloristic depth studies can be cited for American tradition. The tireless and productive Ozark collector Vance Randolph together with George P. Wilson wrote *Down in the Holler: A Gallery of Ozark Folk Speech* (Norman: University of Oklahoma Press, 1953) [PE2970/09R3], an important supplement to Randolph's many works on Ozark folklore. Charles C. Adams's *Boontling: An American Lingo* (Austin: University of Texas Press, 1971) [PE3101/C3A63] documents and analyzes in full detail a contrived jargon—possibly "folk speech"—of a northern California region.

Namelore and its study (onomastics) have received relatively little attention by folklorists, although there are many possibilities for research as outlined in such essays as Robert M. Rennick's "The Folklore of Curious and Unusual Names (A Brief Introduction to the Folklore of Onomastics)," *New York Folklore Quarterly*, 22 (1966), 5–14, and Jan Harold Brunvand's introduction to the "Names in Folklore" special issue of *Names*, 16 (1968), 197–206.

For the proverb we have an erudite general introductory volume by the international authority on the subject, Archer Taylor. His work is titled simply *The Proverb* (Cambridge, Mass.: Harvard University Press, 1931) and may most conveniently be consulted in a reissue, where it appears together with an index first published in 1934 in *FFC* (Hatboro, Pa.: Folklore Associates, 1962) [PN6401/T3]. Organized around origins of proverbs, content of proverbs, style of proverbs, and miscellaneous proverbial types, *The Proverb* sets up the general terms of "paremiology" and cites the basic paremiological literature for literate cultures and mostly in a literary tradition.

Dictionaries of proverbs are numerous, voluminous, but seldom exclusively oral-traditional in their emphasis. A basic work for the English language is William George Smith's *The Oxford Dictionary of English Proverbs* (New York: Oxford University Press, 1935; 3rd rev. ed. G. P. Wilson, 1970) [PN6421/09]. Archer Taylor and Bartlett Jere Whiting's *A Dictionary of American Proverbs and Proverbial Phrases, 1820–1880* (Cambridge, Mass.: Harvard University Press, 1958) [PN6426/T28] culls traditional texts from printed sources, and Frances M. Barbour's *Proverbs and Proverbial Phrases of Illinois* (Carbondale: Southern Illinois University Press, 1965) [PN6426/B3] is a good recent collection drawn from oral tradition.

A traditional text-oriented approach to proverb studies is Margaret M. Bryant's "Proverbs and How to Collect Them," issued as *Publications of the American Dialect Society* (PADS), no. 4, 1945. As noted in Chapter 1, Archer Taylor contributed the lead article—a short useful statement—"The Study of Proverbs" to the first issue of the specialized journal *Proverbium* (1965). A good account of the anthropologically or contextually oriented approach to proverbs is

E. Ojo Arewa and Alan Dundes's "Proverbs and the Ethnography of Speaking Folklore," *American Anthropologist,* 66 (1964), 70–85. Archer Taylor is also the primary older authority on riddles as well as proverbs, and again we may reach for his basic work as an introduction to the field. Taylor's *English Riddles from Oral Tradition* (Berkeley and Los Angeles: University of California Press, 1951) [PN6371/T3] combines a massive classification system with a full index and wide-ranging bibliography. It is the *strategy* of riddling—the cryptic description in terms of something basically unlike the answer, not the answer itself—that is the basis of this ingenious classification, and Taylor explores thoroughly the ramifications of this in introducing the sections of the book. Since riddles themselves are quoted throughout, it is also quite easy to browse through this classificatory work in folklore scholarship.

Archer Taylor's essay "The Riddle," *California Folklore Quarterly,* 2 (1943), 129–147, distinguishes the true folk riddle from the literary riddle (which has a separate learned tradition of its own) and miscellaneous types of "riddling questions," and it sets forth the basic approaches in riddle studies. Taylor and fieldworker Vance Randolph's essay "Riddles in the Ozarks," *Southern Folklore Quarterly,* 7 (1944), 1–10, is a good example of a well-annotated collection of oral texts. For more modern approaches to this genre, see Robert A. Georges and Alan Dundes, "Toward a Structural Definition of the Riddle," *Journal of American Folklore,* 76 (1963), 111–118, and a contextual study, Kenneth S. Goldstein, "Riddling Traditions in Northeastern Scotland," *Journal of American Folklore,* 76 (1963), 330–336.

Terms like "folk rhyme" and "folk poetry" could embrace such a great number and variety of specific types and examples that it is difficult to generalize about them or to select basic references. In addition, most such *texts* belong ideally in their proper *contexts* as work rhymes (cadence counts, planting rhymes, etc.), game rhymes, autograph-book rhymes, or the like. One of the few separate collections of rhymes is Thomas Talley's *Negro Folk Rhymes* (New York: Macmillan, 1922) [PS595/N3T3], which has an interesting variety of material but not much in the way of analysis or comparison. Duncan Emrich's *American Folk Poetry* (Boston: Little, Brown, 1974) [PS593/L8E5] is somewhat mistitled, containing as it does texts exclusively from American ballads and folksongs.

Nursery rhymes, a venerable genre with important oral and literary offshoots, are expertly treated in Iona Opie and Peter Opie's work *The Oxford Dictionary of Nursery Rhymes* (New York: Oxford University Press, 1951) [PZ8.3/060x]. Many works on nursery rhymes purport to explain their "hidden meanings" and "true origins"; only the Opies' work fixes a skeptical eye on all "would-be origin finders" and "happy guessers," as they term them, and explains the material strictly from verifiable historical data. A fruitful source, probably the chief one, of oral versions of nursery rhymes is discussed in C. Grant Loomis's "Mary Had a Parody: A Rhyme of Childhood in Folk Tradition," *Western Folklore,* 17 (1958), 45–51. Modern nursery-rhyme parodies, mostly sexually suggestive ones, are treated in Joseph Hickerson and Alan Dundes, "Mother Goose Vice Verse," *Journal of American Folklore,* 75 (1962), 249–259.

There are good possibilities for research in folk rhymes too numerous for a full listing here. One example of a common form that has seldom been recorded in print is in George G. Carey's "A Collection of Airborne [military parachutists'] Cadence Chants," *Journal of American Folklore,* 78 (1965), 52–61. A useful list and bibliography to guide the beginning student of common childhood rhymes is Roger D. Abrahams's *Jump-Rope Rhymes: A Dictionary* (Austin: University of Texas Press, AFS Bibliographical and Special Series, vol. 20, 1969) [PE1519/A2].

FOLK LITERATURE

Although the expression "folk literature" may seem a contradiction in terms, there is a sense in which oral narratives may be considered the counterpart of printed fiction, or traditional folksongs the counterpart of published poetry and song. Some scholars criticize qualifying the word "literature" with "oral" or "folk" as a "verbal-centric" approach to defining traditional genres; others protest that folk ballads are more "illiterature" than literature. Still, it seems clear that people do *tell* stories or print them, *sing* songs or write them, for much the same reasons—in order to reshape reality in a creative fashion so as to discover meanings in life and to comment on them. Although there are great differences in style, intent, media, audience, and so on between formal and folk literature, the basic storytelling and poetizing impulses behind them are comparable. This is not to suggest, of course, that the approaches to *studying* folktales and folksongs versus art fiction and poetry should be identical; as with all folklore, we must come to these materials on their own terms and not misapply the methods and criteria of literary criticism. If a dilemma such as "Are jokes and broadside ballads worthy of study as folk literature?" troubles you, then drop our handy term and leave "literature" in peace. The labels "folktales" and "ballads and folksongs" will do as well.

Folktales. Stith Thompson's general survey *The Folktale* (New York: Dryden Press, 1946) [PN1001/T5], although outdated in bibliography and other reference material, still remains a useful introduction to the basic problems and approaches of folk narrative study. Apparently composed by oral dictation, the book has an easy, chatty style in which are discussed the complex worldwide history of folk narratives and their equally complicated study in deceptively well-organized fashion. Thompson outlines the forms of folk narratives, traces their distribution "from Ireland to India," and reviews folktale scholarship up to the date of his writing; a long separate section of the book deals with North American Indian folktales. Full documentation, bibliographies, and motif and type indexes of the material discussed make *The Folktale* an invaluable guide to further reading in the comparative approach to folk narrative studies.

Emma Emily Kiefer, a student of Stith Thompson, provided a good summary of the important German and Scandinavian approaches to folktale scholarship in a monograph centered on one individualistic theorist: *Albert Wesselski and Recent Folktale Theories* (Bloomington: Indiana University Folklore Series, no. 3, 1947) [GR40/K5]. A similar review with more time depth is Anna Birgitta Rooth's "Scholarly Tradition in Folktale Research," *Fabula*, 1 (1958), 193–200. The keystone work in the historic-geographic approach—still to be reckoned with today—was Kaarle Krohn's *Die Folkloristische Arbeitsmethode* (1926), available now in Roger L. Welsch's translation from the German, *Folklore Methodology* (Austin, Texas: AFS Bibliographical and Special Series, no. 21, 1971) [GR40/K713]. Besides the many older folktale studies cited in Thompson's book, a later one in the classic European scholarly tradition is Reidar Christiansen's *Studies in Irish and Scandinavian Folktales* (Copenhagen: Rosenkilde and Bagger, 1959) [GR205/C5].

Contemporary departures in folktale scholarship may be located in the earlier section of this chapter on theories or in the later one on text, texture, and context.

The current edition of Antti Aarne's catalogue of European folktale types is Stith Thompson's second revision and expansion titled *The Types of the Folktale* (Helsinki: FFC, no. 184, 1961) [GR1/F55 no. 184]. The *Type-Index* is cross-indexed with Thompson's *Motif-Index of Folk Literature*, 6 vols. (Copenhagen: Rosenkilde and Bagger, 1955–1958) [GR67/T531955], which should be consulted now only in its *second* edition, for many motifs have been reorganized or renumbered since its original publication in the 1930s. Using either of these classifications nearly always necessitates following references back to satellite works such as Baughman's Anglo-American index (see Chapter 1) or Terrence L. Hansen's *The Types of the Folktale in Cuba, Puerto-Rico, Dominican Republic and Spanish South America* (Berkeley and Los Angeles: University of California Folklore Studies, no. 8, 1957) [GR15/C3 no. 8].

Some older folktale reference works have been described in Chapter 1, but a new kind of approach—alphabetically arranged and nationally limited—is represented in Katharine M. Briggs's *A Dictionary of British Folk-Tales in the English Language*. The scope and usefulness of the work were described by the compiler in an essay published in the *Journal of the Folklore Institute*, 2 (1965), 272–275. There are two parts to the *Dictionary*, each comprising two volumes: Pt. A, Folk Narratives (1970) and Pt. B, Folk Legends (1971); both were published in Bloomington by the Indiana University Press [GR141/B69].

Myth is a broad and diversified subject that has various different meanings in studies of folklore, anthropology, literature, and history of religion. Perhaps the best mode of approach for a student who is interested primarily in the myth study in the first two areas is to use collections of essays that offer different points of view, for example, Thomas A. Sebeok's "Myth: A Symposium," *Journal of American Folklore*, 68 (1955), 379–495; of major importance here are Richard M. Dorson's "The Eclipse of Solar Mythology" and Stith Thompson's "Myths and Folktales." A longer compilation, broader in its coverage, is fourteen essays collected on "Myths and Mythmaking," *Daedalus*, 88 (1959), 211–380, edited by Henry A. Murray;

students of folklore will especially appreciate Dorson's contribution "Theories of Myth and the Folklorist" and Clyde Kluckhohn's "Recurrent Themes in Myths and Mythmaking."

For the anthropological viewpoint on myth, a good starting point is Melville Jacobs's special issue of the *Journal of American Folklore,* "The Anthropologist Looks at Myth," 79 (1966), i–305, featuring ten solid studies by leading anthropological folklorists. Robert A. Georges has assembled basic theoretical essays ranging from those by Boas to Lévi-Strauss in an historical context in *Studies on Mythology* (Homewood, Ill.: Dorsey Press, 1968) [BN470/G44]. The student who wishes to read a thorough analysis of a body of myths in the contexts of their own cultural backgrounds, other cultures, and modern myth theories might select Melville J. Herskovits and Frances S. Herskovits's *Dahomean Narrative, a Cross-Cultural Analysis* (Evanston, Ill.: Northwestern University Press, 1958) [DT30/N6].

Because of the rather indeterminate nature of the material, studies of folk legends have advanced more slowly than those for other folk narrative forms. Wayland D. Hand describes the "Status of European and American Legend Study" in *Current Anthropology,* 6 (1965), 439–446; the bibliography here is quite comprehensive. Hand edited an excellent group of papers from a UCLA conference of legend scholars: *American Folk Legend: A Symposium* (Berkeley and Los Angeles: Publications of the UCLA Center for the Study of Comparative Folklore and Mythology, no. 2, 1971) [GR100/U251969].

Perhaps the most perplexing questions of the many puzzles in legend study are "*When* and *how* do beliefs—whether traditional or personal—become true legends?" Beginning with some of C. W. von Sydow's proposed folk narrative terminology, Finnish folklorist Lauri Honko devised a hypothetical flowchart for legend formation to indicate how "narratives of personal happenings" may be influenced by various stimuli to become structured as genuine legendary narrations; see "Memorates and the Study of Folk Beliefs," *Journal of the Folklore Institute,* 1 (1964), 5–19. The latest reaction to Honko's ideas is an important essay by Linda Dégh and Andrew Vázsonyi, "The Memorate and the Proto-Memorate," *Journal of American Folklore,* 87 (1974), 225–239. As both studies clearly demonstrate, although with quite different materials, here as perhaps in no other area of folk narrative study we are often able to observe the very process of generation of new folk traditions going on in the contemporary world.

Two full-fledged folk/literary legend studies deserve to be emulated by other scholars, although the demands on one's linguistic and bibliographic abilities are great. Both are concerned with widespread religious legends: Barbara Allen Woods, *The Devil in Dog Form: A Partial Type-Index of Devil Legends* (Berkeley and Los Angeles: University of California Folklore Studies, no. 11, 1959) [GR15/C3 no. 11], and George K. Anderson, *The Legend of the Wandering Jew* (Providence, R.I.: Brown University Press, 1965) [GR75/W3A5].

In the Old World tradition, hero legends often belong more to literature now than folklore; and in the New World, these legends belong more to fakelore. For a close review of the credentials of a supposed American folk hero, see Daniel G. Hoffman's *Paul Bunyan, Last of the Frontier Demigods* (Philadelphia: University of Pennsylvania Press, 1952; reissued, New York: Columbia University Press, 1966) [PS461/B8H6]. A more authentic and less ballyhooed American hero, riverman and ringtailed roarer Mike Fink, is traced by Walter Blair and Franklin J. Meine in *Half Horse, Half Alligator* (Chicago: University of Chicago Press, 1956) [F353/F5B56]. One recent example of the fully folk but little known hero type, the "regional Münchausen," is taken up by C. Richard K. Lunt in "Jones Tracy: Tall Tale Hero from Mount Desert Island," *Northeast Folklore*, no. 10 (1968), 1–75.

The tall tale itself, a venerable folk form and a particular favorite on the American frontier, is represented in many published books and articles. (The *Type-Index* barely does justice to tall tales, but several major categories are represented in Chapter "X" of the *Motif-Index* under "Exaggerations," and many more are in the corresponding section of Baughman's index.) The tall tale repertoire of a tradition-rich region is gathered in Vance Randolph's *We Always Lie to Strangers: Tall Tales from the Ozarks* (New York: Columbia University Press, 1951) [PS558/A8R3]. Roger Welsch has collected texts from both oral tradition and print in *Shingling the Fog and Other Plains Lies: Tall Tales of the Great Plains* (Chicago: Swallow Press, 1972) [GR109/W4]. Variant texts of tall tales are easily located by following up references in books such as these and in the folk narrative indexes. An important *study* of the form, and one which also introduces a previously unheralded foreign body of material, is Gustav Henningsen's essay "The Art of Perpendicular Lying—Concerning a Commercial Collecting of Norwegian Sailors' Tall Tales," translated from a Norwegian article of 1961 by Warren E. Roberts and published in the *Journal of the Folklore Institute*, 2 (1965), 180–219.

Gradually, jokes as a revealing form of modern folk narrative are coming into their own as a subject for serious study; guidelines and backgrounds for research are set forth in Jan Harold Brunvand, "The Study of Contemporary Folklore: Jokes," *Fabula*, 13 (1972), 1–19. One of the largest printed collections of annotated joke texts is Vance Randolph's *Hot Springs and Hell, and Other Folk Jests and Anecdotes from the Ozarks* (Hatboro, Pa.: Folklore Associates, 1965) [GR110/M77R274], which contains 460 brief oral jests graced with 130 pages of bibliographic and comparative notes. An annotated international sampling of jokes is found in Kurt Ranke, ed., *European Anecdotes and Jests* (Copenhagen: Rosenkilde and Bagger, European Folklore Series, vol. 4, 1972) [GR135/E85]. Further collections, classifications, and studies of various jokes and joke themes abound in the folklore journals, especially those of the past ten years.

Over the years it has been the so-called "fairy tale"—also *Märchen*, wonder tale, magic tale, or "ordinary folktale"—that has held folklorists' and the public's interest the longest. Much of the history of *folklore* studies is really the history of *fairy tale* studies (see Chapter 1). When Stith Thompson writes of "the folktale," this is the kind of narrative he has in mind, and his *Type-Index* is to a large extent an index of *Märchen*.

Three European folktale scholars, Laurits Bødker, Christina Hole, and G. D'Aronco, have edited a good sampler of English translations of genuine *Märchen* texts in *European Folk Tales* (Copenhagen: Rosenkilde and Bagger, European Folklore Series, vol. 1, 1963) [GR135/E85 vol. 1], but the fifty-five tales from twenty countries are a mere drop in the ocean. A larger selection (more like a teaspoon in the ocean) can be found in the series "Folktales of the World," edited by Richard M. Dorson, in which an authority on folktales from each country represented is responsible for securing a book of clear, accurate English translations of a representative body of tales, and then annotating the tales comparatively. Since each volume in the series is keyed to the *Type-Index* and *Motif-Index* and has a glossary and a bibliography, it serves as a partial finding list for that country's tale types. Each published book in the series is titled simply *Folktales of* ———, and most libraries will have a series catalogue card on file as well as separate author, title, and subject listings; most of the volumes have also been issued in paperback editions.

The basic bibliography of published American versions of *Märchen* is contained in Baughman's indispensable index (see above). Merely two outstanding examples of these, among scores, are Vance Randolph, *The Devil's Pretty Daughter and Other Ozark Folktales* with notes by Herbert Halpert (New York: Columbia University Press, 1955) [GR110/M77R27], and Leonard W. Roberts, *South from Hell-fer-Sartin: Kentucky Mountain Folk Tales* (Lexington: University of Kentucky Press, 1955; paperback rpt. Berea, Kentucky: Council of the Southern Mountains, 1964) [GR110/K4R6].

Folktales as *oral* literature cannot be appreciated fully in mere printed representations, but unfortunately very few authentic folk tellings are available on commercial recordings, and even the aural medium cannot present the full dimensions of gesture, expression, and audience reaction. Two outstanding examples of what may be demanded of folktale recordings from many other regions both come from the tradition of a single state: Duncan Emrich, ed., *Jack Tales Told by Mrs. Maud Long of Hot Springs, N.C.* (Washington, D.C.: Library of Congress, AAFS L47, 1957), and Sandy Paton, ed., *Ray Hicks of Beech Mountain, North Carolina, Telling Four Traditional "Jack Tales"* (Huntington, Vt.: Folk-Legacy Records, Inc., FTA-14, 1964). Both recordings are accompanied by printed notes and commentary, and both storytellers are superb performers.

Ballads and Folksongs. The serious collecting and study of traditional ballads and songs predates the formal beginnings of general folklore studies; thus, it is not surprising to find that, with the possible exception of folktales, no other genre of folklore boasts such a rich and diversified bibliography as do narrative and lyrical folksongs. Since English and Anglo-American folk music in particular has been very long and thoroughly studied, selecting a few basic references from the mass of titles is a difficult task. Fortunately, however, with longevity the field has also acquired a certain measure of maturity, and thus there are some reliable surveys, anthologies, and indexes to be recommended.

Two concise overviews by ethnomusicologist Bruno Nettl effectively place into their proper cultural and scholarly contexts the major traditions of folk music likely to be of most interest to beginning students. His book *Folk and Traditional Music of the Western Continents* (Englewood Cliffs, N.J.: Prentice-Hall, 1965) [ML3545/N5] surveys the field under the headings Germanic, Eastern Europe, France, Italy, the Iberian Peninsula, Africa, American Indian, Negroes of the New World, and Western folk music in the Americas. His slight handbook *An Introduction to Folk Music in the United States* (Detroit: Wayne State University Press, 1960; rev. ed., 1962) [ML3551/N471962] takes the narrower view specified in its title but also probes into "Folk Music in the Metropolis" and "The Professional Folk Singer." Both works are replete with musical examples, and both discuss technical aspects of musical analysis in clear, orderly, well-defined terms so that even the lay reader may follow.

The latest definitive history of studies in a major folksong tradition is D. K. Wilgus's highly detailed work *Anglo-American Folksong Scholarship Since 1898* (New Brunswick, N.J.: Rutgers University Press, 1959) [ML3553/W48]. The published histories of "pre-Child" folksong scholarship are cited in Wilgus's introduction, and he ably carries on from that point, reviewing theories, evaluating published works, pointing out gaps, compiling bibliography, and so forth. It is more readable than it sounds, and the complete subject-title index allows easy locating of works on particular folksongs or folksong traditions.

Two recent mini-anthologies ably summarize significant directions in modern folksong scholarship. Roger D. Abrahams edited four survey essays that take, respectively, the literary and aesthetic approach (Tristram P. Coffin), the anthropological approach (John Greenway), the comparative approach (W. Edson Richmond), and the rationalistic approach (D. K. Wilgus). This collection, which has the general heading "Folksong and Folksong Scholarship," closes with "The Transcription and Analysis of Folk Music" by George Foss. It was published in 1964 as *Publications of the Texas Folklore Society* annual, vol. 32, and issued separately in paperback format the same year by Southern Methodist University Press, Dallas, Texas.

Three essays—separate studies of "folk creators" of songs—by Henry Glassie, Edward D. Ives, and John F. Szwed were published in booklet form as *Folksongs and Their Makers* (Bowling Green, Ohio: Bowling Green University Popular Press, 1970) [ML55/G6].

Rich resources are available for the study of English and Anglo-American ballads per se. Good beginning guidance may be found in the anthology *The Critics and the Ballad,* edited by MacEdward Leach and Tristram P. Coffin (Carbondale: Southern Illinois University Press, 1961) [PS476/L4]; in this book, fifteen contributors discuss "Ballad Origins and Ballad Definitions," "The Meter and Music of the Ballad," and "The Ballad and Its Literary Tradition." Two general treatises on the genre that offer essentially the literary viewpoint on ballads are Gordon Hall Gerould's *The Ballad of Tradition* (New York: Oxford University Press, 1932; paperback rpt. New York: Galaxy Books, 1957) [PN1376/G4], and M. J. C. Hodgart's *The Ballads* (London: Hutchinson's University Library, 1950; 2nd. ed., 1962) [PR507/H7]. To widen the scope of national ballad traditions, see William James Entwistle's *European Balladry* (New York: Oxford University Press, 1939) [PN1376/E5].

A leading American folksong scholar, Albert B. Friedman, has traced the influence of folk ballads on sophisticated poetry in English from the eighteenth century to modern times in his book *The Ballad Revival* (Chicago: University of Chicago Press, 1961) [PR507/F85]. Friedman's study recognizes that a major current use of folk ballads in education is "to awaken the uninitiated to the charms of poetry," which is exactly the manner in which many readers of this guide may have first encountered ballads. Friedman himself has edited an anthology of ballads much used in introductory college folklore courses and featuring a varied and well-annotated selection: *The Viking Book of Folk Ballads of the English Speaking World* (New York: Viking Press, 1956; paperback rpt. 1963) [PR1181/F74].

Most ballad surveys concentrate on the classic "Child ballad" canon. An excellent work on the later, more journalistic British street ballads is Claude M. Simpson's *The British Broadside Ballad and Its Music* (New Brunswick, N.J.: Rutgers University Press, 1966) [ML2831/S39]. No single work analyzes solely the native American ballad tradition, but one recent book on the productions of a major group may be cited as a fine example of possibilities in this direction. In 1908 the cowboy-collector N. Howard ("Jack") Thorp put together the first separate anthology of cowboy songs—largely ballads —containing twenty-three texts. It was titled *Songs of the Cowboys* and printed in a cheap pamphlet form to be sold directly by Thorp himself. Recently folklorists Austin E. Fife and Alta S. Fife issued a facsimile edition of this rare publication complete with "variants, commentary, notes, and lexicon" (New York: Clarkson N. Potter, 1966) [ML3551/T43 1966].

There are three essential Anglo-American ballad syllabi that contain survey introductions, classification, bibliography, and some commentary on individual items, all published by the American Folklore Society: G. Malcolm Laws, Jr., *Native American Balladry* (Philadelphia: AFS Bibliographical and Special Series, vol. 1, 1950; reissued, 1964) [GR20/A4 vol. 1, 1964]; Tristram P. Coffin, *The British Traditional Ballad in North America* (Philadelphia: AFS Bibliographical and Special Series, vol. 2, 1950; reissued, 1963) [GR20/A4 vol. 2, 1963]; and G. Malcolm Laws, Jr., *American Balladry from British Broadsides* (Philadelphia: AFS Bibliographical and Special Series, vol. 8, 1957) [GR20/A4 vol. 8].

There are innumerable collections of ballads and folksongs in journals and many book-length anthologies, mostly from individual countries, states, regions, or groups. All of these are easily located through survey works and classifications mentioned above; to take midwestern America simply as a sample area, three solid representative one-volume collections are Emelyn Elizabeth Gardner and Geraldine J. Chickering, *Ballads and Songs of Southern Michigan* (Ann Arbor: University of Michigan Press, 1939; rpt. Hatboro, Pa.: Folklore Associates, 1967) [M1629/G23B18]; H. M. Belden, *Ballads and Songs Collected by the Missouri Folklore Society* (Columbia: University of Missouri Studies, vol. 15, 1940) [AS36/M8 n.s. vol. 15 no. 1]; and Paul Brewster, *Ballads and Songs of Indiana* (Bloomington: Indiana University Folklore Series, no. 1, 1940) [ML3551/B83B2]. All of these have the hallmarks of reliable folklore text publications (sources, comparative notes, bibliography, etc.), and all suffer the common shortcoming of many older books in that they have mostly *textual* variants, with only a nod to the music. A similarly endowed collection from a rich region is Vance Randolph's four-volume *Ozark Folksongs* (Columbia, Mo.: State Historical Society, 1946–1950) [M1629/R2309].

Naturally, folksongs even more than other forms of verbal folklore require the dimension of sound recording rather than the mere printing of them to be fully documented and appreciated. There is, of course, no shortage of folksong recordings, but unfortunately many that purport to or appear to contain genuine traditional music are really personalized professional performances by products of the "folksong revival." Serious students of folk music must apply the same standards of source, text, and annotation to recordings as to books containing folklore; they can find guidance in the record columns and reviews now published in many scholarly folklore journals. The catalogues of records published by the Music Division of the Library of Congress, by Folkways Records, and Folk-Legacy Records are especially recommended; their offerings are most easily acquired by mail order. A good panorama of traditional musical styles from a single state is available in Harry Oster's annotated recording *Folk Voices of Iowa* (Iowa City: University of Iowa Press, 1965).

Most of the aforementioned ballad/folksong references belong largely to the old literary-oriented, text-dominated tradition of folklore scholarship. The gradual shift in American folksong studies to musical and contextual approaches was outlined in Chapter 1, and some major works were identified. Supplementing this beginning, the student might turn to such books as Harry Oster's *Living Country Blues* (Detroit: Folklore Associates, 1969) [ML3561/J3089], the focus of which is self-evident from the title, or to Archie Green's *Only a Miner: Studies in Recorded Coal-Mining Songs* (Urbana: University of Illinois Press, 1972) [ML3780/G74], which takes up where George Korson's collections from coal miners' oral traditions left off. Bill C. Malone's history *Country Music, U.S.A.* (Austin, Texas: AFS Memoir Series, vol. 54, 1968) [GR1/A5 vol. 54] entertainingly but authoritatively takes in "rural southern music of the United States now known as country music, and also variously known as old-time, hillbilly, and country western, and having among its styles honky-tonk, bluegrass and western swing," to quote from the exuberant cover blurb. A revealing overview of the folksong revival by one of its promoters is Oscar Brand's *The Ballad Mongers: Rise of the Modern Folk Song* (New York: Funk & Wagnalls, 1962) [ML3551/B8].

The surveys and histories cited above all call attention to specialists and their publications concerning the *music* of ballads and folksongs. A good notion of the practical problems involved in the analysis of a particular set of materials of folk music may be gained from Jan Philip Schinhan's treatment of the music in the Frank C. Brown Collection (see "Genres" above), which appears in volumes 4 ("The Music of the Ballads") and 5 ("The Music of the Folksongs") of the published material.

The outstanding scholar engaged in studies of Anglo-American ballad music is Bertrand H. Bronson, whose book *The Ballad as Song* (Berkeley and Los Angeles: University of California Press, 1969) [ML3553/B76], which reprints essays and reviews, is some help— although highly technical—in approaching his ongoing definitive treatment *The Traditional Tunes of the Child Ballads* (Princeton, N.J.: Princeton University Press, vol. 1, 1959, vol. 2, 1962, and continuing) [ML3650/B82].

A purely *musical* American tradition (except for some floating and highly variable stanzas occasionally sung with the music) consists of dance tunes for the fiddle. A pioneering study of fiddle tunes is Samuel P. Bayard's *Hill Country Tunes: Instrumental Folk Music of Southwestern Pennsylvania* (Philadelphia: AFS Memoirs, vol. 39, 1944) [GR1/A5 vol. 39]. Ira W. Ford's large published collection of American fiddle tunes *Traditional Music of America* (1940) has long been difficult to acquire, but it has been reissued with an introduction by Judith McCulloh (Hatboro, Pa.: Folklore Associates, 1965) [M1629/F69T71965].

BELIEFS, CUSTOMS, AND GAMES

Space limitations do not allow for even a cursory review of the whole bibliography of customary folklore, what might be called "traditional folkways." Bibliographies, textbooks, histories, and surveys already cited may be consulted for information about such forms as folk dances, dramas, festivals, and gestures. Here we shall attempt only a brief review of publications that are helpful in studying folk beliefs (or "superstitions"), folk customs, and folk games.

Wayland D. Hand's system of classification used for the beliefs and superstitions in the Frank C. Brown collection (volumes 6 and 7 of the published work) has been followed in several other published collections and has proved useful for archiving purposes, although it divorces beliefs from their functional contexts. The Brown collection, drawn from North Carolina alone, does not necessarily contain samples of every kind of folk belief, but representation is quite broad among its more than 8,000 entries. Hand has annotated these thoroughly and provided a lengthy bibliography and a good introductory essay on the nature of folk beliefs and their study. Among other compilations of folk beliefs the student should compare Vance Randolph's *Ozark Superstitions* (New York: Columbia University Press, 1947; rpt. New York: Dover Books, 1964) [GR110/A8R3], in which the material is placed in a narrative context, and Ray B. Browne's *Popular Beliefs and Practices from Alabama* (Berkeley and Los Angeles: University of California Folklore Studies, no. 9, 1958) [GR15/C3 no. 9], which has items arranged in a dictionary format.

Witchcraft in Anglo-American tradition is discussed by the famous literary scholar and sometime folklorist George Lyman Kittredge in *Witchcraft in Old and New England* (Cambridge, Mass.: Harvard University Press, 1929) [BF1581/K58]. This is probably the best place to begin one's reading in this area since so many of the numerous treatises on witchcraft are written by devotees and alleged practitioners rather than scholars. Water witching—locating underground sources of water by magical means—is totally unrelated to witchcraft proper, but it is sometimes confused with it because of the similar name. A thorough investigation of this traditional practice (also called "dowsing") is Evon Z. Vogt and Ray Human's *Water Witching U.S.A.* (Chicago: University of Chicago Press, 1959) [BF1628/V6].

Virtually all survey texts in folklore devote ample attention to folk beliefs and their study, and the folklore journals are liberally supplied with specialized investigations. Two of the latter that are unusually speculative and interesting are Eric Berne's "The Mythology of Dark and Fair: Psychiatric Use of Folklore," *Journal of American Folklore,* 72 (1959), 1–13; and Alan Dundes, "The Folklore of Wishing Wells," *American Imago,* 19 (1962), 27–34. Possibly as a counterweight against these two very speculative essays, but certainly as a good example of a contextual approach, students may turn to Patrick B. Mullen's "The Function of Magic Folk Belief among Texas Coastal Fishermen," *Journal of American Folklore,* 82 (1969), 214–225.

A beautiful book combining folk beliefs and customs with historical, religious, and artistic perspectives—all in broad international contexts—is Venetia Newall's lavishly illustrated *An Egg at Easter,*

A Folklore Study (Bloomington: Indiana University Press, 1971) [GR735/N4]. The English Folklore Society publications, such as the collections of "calendar customs" and the various county collections, are rich sources of miscellaneous information on old folk customs. Such recent works as Enid Porter's *Cambridgeshire Customs and Folklore* (London: Routledge & Kegan Paul, 1969) [GR142/C3P6] carry on in that tradition, although in a much more sophisticated comparative approach than most earlier works. In American folklore we have nothing quite comparable to these English products; Paul G. Brewster's treatment of customs in the published Frank C. Brown North Carolina collection (vol. 1, pp. 221–282) may be examined as a fair sample of possibilities, and the general folklore survey texts all touch on customs.

Holiday celebrations are rich in folk backgrounds and practices and yield many possibilities for interesting folklore studies. Two good general reference sources are Robert Chambers's *The Book of Days*, 2 vols. (1862–1864; reissued Philadelphia: Lippincott, 1914) [DA110/C52 1914] and George William Douglas's *The American Book of Days* (1938, 2nd rev. ed. by Helen Douglas Compton, New York: H. W. Wilson, 1948) [GT4803/D6 1948]. George R. Stewart's chapter on holidays in *American Ways of Life* (Garden City, N.Y.: Doubleday, 1954) [E169.1/S84] is highly readable and most suggestive of good projects. John E. Baur's book *Christmas on the American Frontier, 1800–1900* (Caldwell, Idaho: Caxton Printers, 1961) [BT4985/B34] traces the borrowing and alterations of European Christmas customs through historical sources on frontier life.

Several good studies have pursued adaptations of holiday traditions in a new setting. Svatava Pirkova-Jakobson's essay "Harvest Festivals Among Czechs and Slovaks in America," *Journal of American Folklore*, 69 (1956), 266–280 is a model of research and reveals the typical transition of Old World ritual to New World dramatic spectacle. Beatrice S. Weinreich discusses "The Americanization of Passover" in an essay in *Studies in Biblical and Jewish Folklore*, edited by Raphael Patai, Francis Lee Utley, and Dov Noy (AFS Memoir, no. 51; Indiana University Folklore Series, no. 13, 1960, pp. 329–366) [GR1/A5 vol. 51]. David W. Plath investigates Americanized European holiday customs in yet another new permutation in his essay "The Japanese Popular Christmas: Coping with Modernity," *Journal of American Folklore*, 76 (1963), 309–317.

A special study of occupational customs (*sometimes* treated in general books on occupational folklore) is Henning Henningsen's *Crossing the Equator: Sailors' Baptisms and Other Initiation Rites* (Copenhagen: Munksgaard, 1961) [BR910/H43].

Traditional games and recreations, in particular the folk games of children, have enjoyed a tremendously long and varied oral circulation and continue to flourish in modern times hardly touched by the influence of print or mass culture. Folklorists have collected large numbers of game descriptions and texts and devised a few methods of classification, but have not until quite recently subjected much of this material to close analysis. Ironically, many of today's adults (even parents) seem hardly aware of the rich children's folklore that exists all around them in the form of games and rhymes, even in a society devoted to compulsory free public schooling, planned recreations, and television.

A classic early collection of games—one of the first published studies in American folklore—is W. W. Newell's *Games and Songs of American Children* (1883; rpt. from 1903 ed. New York: Dover Books, 1963) [GV1203/N53 1963]. Although somewhat romantic in attitude and (for modern tastes) excessively oriented toward mythological interpretations, Newell did provide important early evidence for the existence and variations of children's games involving verses and song, and he worked out topical groupings such as love games, humor and satire, the pleasures of motion, guessing games, and so on. His work's counterpart in Great Britain was Alice Bertha Gomme's two-volume *The Traditional Games of England, Scotland, and Ireland* (1894, 1898; rpt. New York: Dover Books, 1964) [GR141/G5 1964], which has an alphabetical arrangement but commentaries and interpretations akin to Newell's.

In a good modern example, Paul Brewster edits, classifies, annotates and comments upon children's games in the *Frank C. Brown Collection of North Carolina Folklore*, vol. 1. Brewster deals with the kinds of games Newell ignored, plus many modern ones unknown to Newell's time, in his book *American Nonsinging Games* (Norman: University of Oklahoma Press, 1953) [BV1203/B68].

A detailed study of an individual category of games is Erwin

Mehl's essay (translated from German) "Baseball in the Stone Age," *Western Folklore,* 7 (1948), 145–161. Mehl suggests that games based on the action of batting a ball may actually be identified in history thousands of years ago and have evolved in various ways toward their modern forms. Other comparative and historical studies of games may be found in the survey chapters of textbooks already described. A more innovative approach is represented by Alan Dundes's "On Game Morphology: A Study of the Structure of Non-Verbal Folklore," *New York Folklore Quarterly,* 20 (1964), 276–288. A personal selection of his own and some collaborative studies of children's games seen from anthropological and psychological perspectives is in Brian Sutton-Smith's valuable book *The Folkgames of Children* (Austin: University of Texas Press, AFS Bibliographical and Special Series, No. 24, 1972) [GR1204.91/S79].

FOLKLIFE

The material aspects of folk culture—folk architecture, arts, crafts, costumes, and foods—have long been studied by European folklife scholars and are increasingly attracting the attention of American folklorists. The most recent textbooks, such as Brunvand's *The Study of American Folklore* and Dorson's *Folklore and Folklife,* have substantial sections devoted to material culture; folklife studies are now regularly presented in folklorists' scholarly journals and professional meetings. This is an area of interest that folklorists share with ethnographers, cultural geographers, and museum curators, among others, and thus many folklife specialists and their studies have an interdisciplinary nature. Don Yoder, a leading American folklife scholar with special interests in Pennsylvania German sectarian costume puts the field in historical and academic perspectives in "The Folklife Studies Movement," *Pennsylvania Folklife,* 13 (July 1963), 43–56.

An extremely useful survey of publications in American folklife prepared by a leading European specialist, Robert Wildhaber, director of the folklife museum in Basel, Switzerland, is "A Bibliographical Introduction to American Folklife," published in *New York Folklore Quarterly,* 21 (1965), 259–320. Wildhaber confined his selections mostly to books, but he does give the titles of relevant periodicals and offers astute evaluations of works, trends, accomplishments, and failings of American folklife scholarship and publications. A fine example of a European folklife survey is E. Estyn Evans's well-illustrated ethnography of rural Irish life and traditions, *Irish Folk Ways* (New York: Devin-Adair, 1957) [GR147/E9 1957a]. A sampling of recent British and European folklife research is gathered in Geraint Jenkins's anthology *Studies in Folk Life* (New York: Barnes & Noble, 1969) [GR70/S77 1969b]; these twenty studies were published to honor Iorwerth C. Peate, curator of the Welsh Folk Museum and first president of the Society for Folk Life Studies (publishers of the journal *Folk Life*), and a bibliography of Peate's own studies is included.

Leonard W. Roberts's *Up Cutshin and Down Greasy: Folkways of a Kentucky Mountain Family* (Lexington: University of Kentucky Press, 1959) [F451/R6] is a folklife survey in a regional and family context; it was issued together with a microcard edition of one hundred folktales and sixty-six folksongs from the family involved. A very readable essay describing the folklife scene in a Western setting is Louie Attebery's "Rural Traditions of the Snake River Valley [Idaho]," *Northwest Folklore*, 1 (1966), 23–30.

The most ambitious *analytical* work in American folklife so far to appear is Henry Glassie's *Pattern in the Material Folk Culture of the Eastern United States* (Philadelphia: University of Pennsylvania Monographs in Folklore and Folklife, no. 1, 1969) [GR105/G56]. Glassie attempts to arrive at a definition of "folk culture" appropriate to the United States and its rapid, highly industrial development; he delves deeply, via numerous examples, into the present interrelations of folk and popular culture. His conclusions about methodology for such studies, the movement of ideas, and the major regions of Eastern American folk culture are important for all such future studies. Glassie's bibliography is detailed and extensive, but unfortunately his treatise lacked a subject index in its first edition, a shortcoming corrected in later printings. A good collection of shorter studies in American folklife edited by Glassie and the Utah folklorists Austin Fife and Alta Fife is "Forms Upon the Frontier: Folklife and Folk Arts in the United States," *Utah State University Monograph Series*, 16 (April 1969) [S537/U885 vol. 16, no. 2].

Although they are not direct offshoots of the professional American folklife movement, many popularized treatments of traditional arts and crafts offer some documentary value to folklorists. For example, Robert Paul Smith's charming book *How to Do Nothing With Nobody, All Alone by Yourself* (New York: W. W. Norton, 1958) [GV1203/S63] takes a nostalgic look at some of the pastimes and casual recreations of American childhood. The title is unwittingly ironic, since these are the traditions of a folk-group culture, not just individual inventions; and, of course, they really need not be taught to children themselves, but only to forgetful adults. The best-selling *Foxfire Book* and its sequel *Foxfire 2* (Garden City, N.Y.: Doubleday, 1972 and 1973) [S521.5/G4F6] were edited by Eliot Wigginton, a rural Georgia high school English teacher who encouraged his students originally to collect the folkways of their surrounding culture to publish their reports in the school periodical, *Foxfire*. Although their publications are without scholarly annotations or discussion, their fieldwork was diligent and their reports are both accurate and beautifully illustrated with photographs and drawings. Unfortunately, the *Foxfire* concept of folklore, which has won generous grant support, relies on the old stereotypes of backwoods rustics whose last shreds of tradition must be rescued before they vanish.

STUDIES OF TEXTURE, TEXT, AND CONTEXT

One systematic description of the varieties of possible approaches to studies in folklore is offered by Alan Dundes in "Texture, Text and Context," *Southern Folklore Quarterly*, 28 (1964), 251–265. Dundes asserts that until the subject matter of folklore is adequately defined in terms of specific *internal* criteria, folklore as a discipline will not advance far. He identifies three levels of analysis that should lead to precise definitions of individual genres, which then might be simply enumerated in order to define the whole realm of folklore. These approaches (or qualities of folklore) he calls *texture*, the linguistic or stylistic level; *text*, the individual version of folklore normally collected and published by folklorists; and *context*, the specific social situations in which items of folklore are performed. Because Dundes identifies exemplary published studies in these three modes and offers his own three-way interpretations of some newly collected materials, the essay is a good introduction to recent folklore research and offers a workable outline for reviewing further studies.

The level of text analysis, which generally comes to text publication, is the usual standard of past research. Innumerable books and essays consist of the verbatim printed texts of oral folklore; they are sometimes supplied with comparative annotations, informant data, and general background notes. A work such as Clifton Johnson's *What They Say in New England and Other American Folklore* (1896; rpt. New York: Columbia University Press, 1963) [GR106/ J5 1963], for example, simply organizes tidbits of lore and language under such headings as "The Weather," "Fortune Telling," "Money," "Death," and "The Moon." As Carl Withers, the editor of the recent edition of the book, writes, Johnson's book is a "charming and classic regional collection of folk sayings, superstitions, children's rhymes and other pastimes, songs, legends and folktales"; but *textural* analysis is left to the reader, and *contextual* information is mostly lacking.

Most modern publications of folklore texts hold to a standard more like that in Richard M. Dorson's *Negro Folktales in Michigan* (Cambridge, Mass.: Harvard University Press, 1956) [GR103/D6]. Here too the emphasis is on the words of the tales, which are arranged in categories like "Old Marster and John," "Witches and Wonders," "Preachers," and "Fairy Tales." Dorson's appended notes supply bibliography, comparative information on analogues, and indexes of informants, motifs, and tale types. But prefatory to the collection itself, Dorson fills in the details of context ("The Communities and the Storytellers") and texture ("The Art of Negro Storytelling"). A similar presentation done in more detail is Daniel J. Crowley's study *I Could Talk Old-Story Good: Creativity in Bahamian Folklore* (Berkeley and Los Angeles: University of California Folklore Studies, no. 17, 1966) [GR15/C3 no. 17], in which the total body of tale texts themselves is not printed, but only statistical summaries, representative passages, and selected examples introduced in the analysis.

An outstanding textural study in American folklore is Richard M. Dorson's essay "Oral Styles of American Folk Narrators," which was originally published in Thomas A. Sebeok, ed., *Style in Language* (New York: Technology Press of M.I.T., 1960), pp. 27–53

[PN203/C6 1958]. A more conveniently available and slightly longer version of the piece is in Dorson's *Folklore: Selected Essays,* mentioned above with other survey works. First, Dorson discusses seven folk narrators from his fieldwork; then, he applies the approach used for analyzing their oral style to Abraham Lincoln's storytelling via the rich published material on him. In general terms, Dorson concludes, American oral storytellers do seem to conform to Axel Olrik's "epic laws" for folk narrative behavior.

Studies limited to close analysis of purely stylistic features of folklore are not common. Except for metrical and some musical or literary studies of ballads, for instance, an essay such as James H. Jones's "Commonplace and Memorization in the Oral Tradition of the English and Scottish Popular Ballads," *Journal of American Folklore,* 74 (1961), 97–112, is a rarity. Jones has attempted to apply the Parry/Lord oral-formulaic thesis developed in minstrel epic and Homeric studies to the Anglo-American folk ballads, an approach sharply criticized by Albert B. Friedman in a counterstatement published in the same issue of *JAF* (pp. 113–115). A more comprehensive treatment of textural features of folksongs is found in Roger D. Abrahams and George Foss's book *Anglo-American Folksong Style* (Englewood Cliffs, N.J.: Prentice-Hall, 1968) [ML3553/A27]. The oral-formulaic approach is applied in great detail and most convincingly to materials from American folklore in Bruce A. Rosenberg's *The Art of the American Folk Preacher* (New York: Oxford University Press, 1970) [BV4208/U6R67].

An introduction to the *contextual* approach to folklore studies, surely the most important recent development in research on folk traditions, is given in Roger Abrahams's "Folklore in Culture: Notes Toward an Analytic Method," *Texas Studies in Language and Literature,* 5 (1963), 98–110. After evaluating different approaches, Abrahams advocates viewing folklore primarily in its proper social and cultural contexts and making use of whatever points of view will illuminate meanings, for, as he writes, "salvation lies in eclecticism."

Two important earlier essays on folklore in context deserve to be read in connection with all the many writings from the "contextual school" now appearing (see "Theories" above); these are William Hugh Jansen's "A Culture's Stereotypes and Their Expression in Folk Clichés," *Southwestern Journal of Anthropology,* 13 (1957),

184–200, and "The Esoteric-Exoteric Factor in Folklore," *Fabula*, 2 (1959), 205–211. The latter piece discusses "what one group thinks of itself and what it supposes others think of it [and] what one group thinks of another and what it thinks that other group thinks it thinks" as expressed in folklore; fortunately, the examples are much clearer than the complex wording necessary for the definition might suggest, and the approach Jansen advocates was widely adopted in many later studies. The essay was reprinted with editor's commentary in Dundes's *The Study of Folklore* (see "Surveys," above).

A major work that attempts to relate textural and contextual features of folklore through an approach dubbed "cantometrics" is Alan Lomax's *Folk Song Style and Culture* (Washington, D.C.: American Association for the Advancement of Science, pub. no. 88, 1968) [ML3545/L63]. One of the clearest and most convincing attempts to turn folktale scholarship away from texts to studies of contexts is Robert A. Georges's "Toward an Understanding of Storytelling Events," *Journal of American Folklore*, 82 (1969), 313–328.

STUDIES OF FOLK GROUPS

Many folklore studies, it might be said, center on the *folk* rather than the *lore*; that is, they emphasize the carriers, performers, and possessors of folklore—the "informants" and "folk groups," as we tend to call them—not the technical aspects of the folklore texts themselves. To conclude this bibliographic survey, we may list some representative studies of groups whose folklore has been presented in this mode.

A folk group, some folklorists suggest, is any group that has some shared traditions—as large as a nation, as small as a nuclear family. Most groups conceived of as *folk* groups, however, have tended to be regional (Ozark residents), religious (Pennsylvania "Dutch," or Mennonites), ethnic (Basque-Americans), or interconnected by national background, family, occupation, hobby, or the like. An outstanding early survey of social-behavioral traditions and folk beliefs of an ethnic group is Phyllis H. Williams's *South Italian Folkways in Europe and America: A Handbook for Social Workers, Visiting Nurses, School Teachers, and Physicians* (New Haven, Conn.: Yale

University Press, 1938) [E184/I8W6]. Peter Opie and Iona Opie, however, have established the cohesiveness, through its oral traditions, of an *age* group—that of schoolchildren—as in their work *The Lore and Language of Schoolchildren,* cited in Chapter 1. Their further study *Children's Games in Street and Playground* (New York: Oxford University Press, 1969) [GV1203/O6] is a fascinating account of the traditional recreations that British children engage in and transmit to each other almost entirely apart from the world of adults.

Members of small and geographically concentrated religious groups often share certain esoteric traditions of lore and behavior. A prime American example of such a group is the Mormons (or Latter-day Saints) of Utah. They have been fully explored in terms of their folklore in Austin E. Fife and Alta Fife's *Saints of Sage and Saddle* (Bloomington: Indiana University Press, 1956) [BX8611/F5] as well as in numerous articles by the Fifes and others. Mormon folklore includes songs of the westward movement, legends of miracles and heroism, pioneer crafts, historical jokes and anecdotes, dialect terms, and many customs and general folkways. Many revealing collections and studies of Pennsylvania German, Southwestern Mexican, and Louisiana Cajun folklore—much of it related to religious themes—have been made; see Dorson's *Buying the Wind* (described under "Folklore Genres," above) for samples and bibliography. An outstanding study from another religious group is Jerome R. Mintz's *Legends of the Hasidim: An Introduction to Hasidic Culture and Oral Tradition in the New World* (Chicago: University of Chicago Press, 1968) [BM198/M52].

Occupational-group folklore has centered on such trades of hardy males as logging, seafaring, cattle herding, railroading, and coal mining, although a search of the survey works and bibliographies in folklore will also turn up scattered studies of the likes of folklore of military personnel, crafts workers, and even academics. Two good representative studies of occupational folklore are George Korson's collection *Black Rock: Mining Folklore of the Pennsylvania Dutch* (Baltimore: Johns Hopkins Press, 1960) [GR900/K65], and Mody C. Boatright's more analytical work *Folklore of the Oil Industry* (Dallas: Southern Methodist University Press, 1963) [TN872/A5B6].

Although American Indian studies have been more the province of anthropologists than folklorists, it is important to give at least a modicum of guidance to students who may wish to find their way through the voluminous published materials to a few leading examples of the special viewpoint of folklore research. In this regard, a useful tool is Judith C. Ullom's bibliography *Folklore of the North American Indians* (Washington, D.C.: Library of Congress, 1969) [Z1209/U4], which offers selected lists of source books and children's editions of Indian folklore as well as materials relating to the various Indian culture areas. (It should also be remembered that Haywood's bibliography, already cited, includes North American Indian references.)

Dorson discusses relations between Indians and whites as reflected in folklore from colonial times on in his textbook *American Folklore,* and he supplies basic references for going further with the subject. The standard compilation of Indian narratives from a folkloristic point of view is Stith Thompson's *Tales of the North American Indians* (1929; paperback ed. Bloomington: Indiana University Press, 1966) [E98/F6T32 1966]. Thompson includes not only material from the native repertoire, but also folktales borrowed from Europe, including some Bible stories. Alan Dundes demonstrates his proposal for a new structural typology of Indian narratives by analyzing a group of samples in *The Morphology of North American Indian Folktales (Folklore Fellows Communications,* no. 195, 1964). He reopens the subject of American ethnic-group borrowings of folk narrative themes from a new perspective in "African Tales Among the North American Indians," *Southern Folklore Quarterly,* 29 (1965), 207–219.

Studies in black American folklore date back to the earliest folklorists in the United States and have continued to be pursued with vigor and theoretical ferment ever since. The published literature, as well as the rich field materials still collectable, offer many opportunities for student research. For the African backgrounds of Anglo-American narrative folklore see Ruth Finnegan's *Oral Literature in Africa* (New York:Oxford University Press, 1970) [PL8010/ F5]. The anthology *African Folklore* (Bloomington: Indiana University Press, 1972) [GR350/D76], edited by Richard M. Dorson, contains sixteen studies of African folk narratives, oral histories, traditional poetry, and rituals. Alan Dundes's compilation *Mother Wit from the Laughing Barrel: Readings in the Interpretation of*

Afro-American Folklore (Englewood Cliffs, N.J.: Prentice-Hall, 1973) [GR103/D86] contains excellent selections of analytical essays in black folklore along with suggestions for further reading.

Three books on black folklore by Bruce Jackson help to establish the full historical dimensions of the subject. His *The Negro and His Folklore in Nineteenth-Century Periodicals* (Austin, Texas: AFS Bibliographical and Special Series, vol. 18, 1967) [GR103/J3] brings together essays from original sources not easily found in many libraries. At the other extreme, his *Wake Up Dead Man: Afro-American Worksongs from Texas Prisons* (Cambridge, Mass.: Harvard University Press, 1972) [M1977/C55J2] draws its materials from present oral tradition, as does his latest work, a study of the black tradition of "toasts," *Get Your Ass in the Water and Swim Like Me* (Cambridge, Mass.: Harvard University Press, 1974) [PS477.5/T6J3].

CHAPTER THREE
The Research Paper

❦ ❦ ❦ Essentially, research is a matter of gathering and evaluating information in order to be able to draw reasonable conclusions. We all perform some research daily as we weigh evidence from different sources and decide on products to buy, courses to take, careers to follow, causes to promote, or candidates to vote for. To prepare a research paper, one must merely organize these common procedures and put them in a formal written argument to support a particular point of view. Such papers are widely used devices in higher education, and they are assigned with the aim of developing students' critical, investigatory, reasoning, and writing skills in relation to a particular subject through a project of individual research.

For many students, however, the research paper has a bad image; it seems like the monstrous invention of some perverse academic mentality that assumes education has to be grim and grueling in order to be effective. Some students search the catalogue and canvass the campus looking for courses that do not require a term paper. Their goal (seldom achieved) is to graduate without having written the dreaded research paper.

Presumably, this guide need not convince you to take up writing a research paper in folklore; if you have read this far, you are already involved. The message, instead, is that there is no reason why you might not actually *enjoy* preparing a research paper in folklore, for the subject has great built-in appeal. Folklore offers such intriguing raw materials, such boundless opportunities for interesting subjects, and so much potential relevance to other fields that only a dedicated academic cynic can remain indifferent to it. Research in folklore is no easier than in many other subjects, but at least it is seldom boring.

Nevertheless, one should not delude oneself that just because much folk material is enjoyable, *research* in folklore means merely collecting and appreciating amusing odds and ends. As with any field of study, the process of research requires careful formulation of a suitable problem to be investigated, orderly accumulation of data, review of what has been done previously, and final production of well-documented and well-reasoned written conclusions. Good research in folklore should be as rigorous and thorough as in any other scholarly endeavor, and the intellectual rewards can be just as great.

The common complaint among undergraduates that there is nothing new to say about a subject hardly applies to folklore, for by definition it is a field that investigates ever-new, constantly varying, and evolving materials. The claim that research papers are nothing but siftings and restatements of others' words carries little weight here either, because students can easily find subjects that lead them out of the library and into the field where they can collect their own data. Furthermore, as previously shown, the scholarly field of folklore is relatively young and still much involved in debates, so that many important theoretical questions have barely been formulated, let alone settled. With judicious choice of a topic and approach, it is possible for even beginning folklorists to make some minor contribution to knowledge, and in the process they will certainly expand their own understanding of how tradition operates in culture.

Beyond the usual scholarly apparatus of published sources and footnotes, folklore research may involve one in such activities as field collecting, transcription of tapes, sketching, or photography, and in borrowing ideas and methods from historians, psychologists, musicologists, and other outside authorities. Research in folklore also requires some familiarity with the specialized terminology, reference works, and theories that are briefly set forth in this guide. With this book in hand, then, and turning to the texts, surveys, bibliographies, periodicals, and studies that it describes, you are well prepared to venture into the closer study of folklore, however new the field may be in your academic experience.

The precise direction and form of your research project will depend a great deal upon the subject and requirements of the course for which the paper is being written. Obviously, the student should consult with the instructor about specific subject matter, length, format, style, and approach in his or her paper. But a successful and fulfilling piece of research should also have real meaning and importance to *you*, and most instructors are grateful for students who can propose valid, interesting, well-defined topics on their own. Then the instructor can easily teach the details of whatever variations of note taking, outlining, or documentation he prefers.

A systematic method of research is of primary importance, especially in the harried world of undergraduate education where time is short and distractions are many. Getting the project started right and keeping it always moving ahead will go a long way toward retaining your peace of mind about it and insuring your success. Have your topic approved early, and be prepared to put considerable time and effort into completing it on time. Some regularly allotted work time each day is better for most people than a crash effort at the last moment. (You may wish to set up personal deadlines for stages of the project, or your instructor may designate them for the whole class.) Learn at the outset how to use the resources of your own college library in the most efficient way. Form the habit as you work of always taking down full, correct, *legible* information on every source that you consult. Always use the existing scholarly guides, for there is no sense in redoing research that others have already done and published.

The final result of your research—whether it begins as fieldwork, a library project, or a theoretical question—will be a formal piece of writing whose main appeal is intellectual. The paper should be focused on a single topic, concisely written, and fully documented. It should be clear and self-contained, so as to be interesting and meaningful to any intelligent reader. If the research has been planned and carried out thoughtfully, the paper should almost write itself in the end. Therefore, a good start on the project is as important as the last proofreading of the finished paper.

SELECTING A TOPIC

The one certain way to court disaster in a research paper—and the sure sign of a rank beginner in any field of research—is to try to write a short report on a topic suitable only for book-length or multivolume treatment. In folklore, for example, don't try to write on "The History of Witchcraft," "The Origin of Superstitions," or "The Meanings of Fairy Tales." Before anything else you must concentrate your attention on a specific, limited subject, usually best expressed as a question to be answered, a hypothesis to be tested, or a small number of folk items (perhaps only one) to be described and discussed.

Usually, the instructor of any course requiring a research paper has a list of suitable topics, and he or she will give you adequate guidance on selecting and developing one. Especially if you are a neophyte in folklore research, you should seriously consider taking one of these topics, and you should also trust your instructor to set you on the right course to find published materials on the recommended subject. Lacking this advice, however, or if you are more adventurous, you can easily find a topic of particular value and interest to you.

The best place to begin looking for a topic for folklore research is in your own life. If you have a distinctive national or ethnic background, for example, general areas ready-made for you might be the likes of German-American Christmas customs, urban blacks' frustrations expressed in jokes, or folk fallacies about Canada. An interesting, talkative older family member might direct your attention to subjects that he or she is an unwitting "authority" on, such as quilt patterns, pioneer tall tales, lore of the Great Depression, or traditions of the railroad. Your own peer group may have folklore that you could study—fraternity legends, athletic superstitions, parodies of good advice and scripture, or the like. Even children in the family or neighborhood could provide your topic; for example, you might become interested in how they choose "It" for games, what toys they make for themselves out of scraps and seeds, or how they represent authority figures like parents and teachers in their traditional songs, games, and rhymes.

Your hobbies, part-time employment, career plans, and especially your college major subject may lead to a good topic. A music student might collect traditional mnemonic devices of beginning musicians ("Every good boy does fine," etc.) or study anecdotes about eccentric opera singers, orchestra conductors, or composers. A student preparing to be a teacher could critique a school encyclopedia article on folklore or else prepare his or her own teaching unit for a subject such as introducing poetry to fourth graders via the poetic qualities of their own jump-rope rhymes. Business majors might write on department store legends, the use of folklore in advertising, or attitudes toward commerce and economics revealed in proverbial sayings like "Business is business," "Money talks," and "Take care of the pennies and the dollars will take care of themselves."

English majors (likely users of this guide) have a broad range of subjects available to them within their field, both in linguistic and literary approaches. Folk speech and naming might be studied either in the context of literature (especially in regional or local-color writing) or in field investigations of local dialects. Stylistic approaches to literary analysis can be used to study folk materials and might yield possible subjects like metaphors in riddles, flower imagery in ballads, or rhetorical "punctuation" (pauses, gestures, repetitions, imitative sounds, etc.) in oral style. One might analyze, as in a literary study, examples of particular themes expressed in such forms of folklore as sayings, graffiti, anecdotes, or folksongs; specific subjects could include male chauvinism, attitudes toward government, or assumptions about the values of education reflected in modern American folklore. And, of course, there are innumerable subjects available dealing with the use of, or the imitation of, folklore by authors.

None of the topics suggested thus far is fully defined, nor would you be ready to write on any of them without a good deal of further specification. The precise narrowing of a general subject down to the dimensions of a problem suitable for a research paper will have to be done as you get into the research itself. In other words, the subject takes final shape only as you work on it, so the important thing at first is simply to get started.

You begin, say, with an interest in "Folklore in Shakespeare," but it is readily apparent that this topic won't do unless you are going to write a ten-volume lifetime masterpiece. "Folk Ballads in Shakespeare," you learn from some reading in the Shakespeare and the ballad scholarship, is still too broad. Look, instead, for a particular play and a single ballad or a kind of ballad. Do not try to write on "Macbeth's Witches," but try perhaps "Macbeth's Witches' Charms" and study their relationship to charms in folk tradition. Even this may eventually end up as "Eye of Newt: Its Role in Literature and Folk Magic." Perhaps you should get away entirely from established Shakespearean authorities; after all, practically none of them has any experience with folklore anyway. How about taking a line from a play such as "Something is rotten in the state of Denmark" and doing a study of how one bit of Shakespeare is quoted, misquoted, and understood in oral tradition?

Surveys and textbooks in folklore are excellent sources of ideas for research topics. One high school teacher wrote the author of this guide to say that she had found more than eighty different subjects for papers in his *The Study of American Folklore* and that she was mimeographing the list for use by her students. (For instance, the last paragraph of the last chapter in the book offers a potpourri of ideas for research in "traditional eating and drinking habits in the United States.")

At the end of Robert J. Smith's "Festivals and Celebrations" in Dorson's *Folklore and Folklife: An Introduction,* the author suggests that "the student might do well at this point to take a look at his own life and the part festivals have played and continue to play in it" (p. 171). Other thought-provoking generalizations from the same article include: "What distinguishes traditional games and recreations from all others is really the method of transmitting rules" (p. 184), and "Popular medicine is in a sense folk medicine gone commercial" (p. 192). In Henry Glassie's essay "Folk Art" in the same book, he states: "All artifacts have more than one function" (p. 253). Glassie makes a case for "bilateral symmetry" as a prime characteristic of folk design, a contention that a student might test against his or her own observations.

The student lucky enough to possess or have access to an artifact from the folk tradition such as a log cabin, an heirloom quilt, or a homemade musical instrument could do a good report by thoroughly describing the object and writing an essay that places it in its traditional and historical context. Students who commute to campus might document a range of modern traditional artifacts within a region, such as fences, rural mail-box supports, or children's tree houses. Local field trips might be made to study traditional gravestones and epitaphs, the oral lore of a National Guard unit, traditions of foreign students (such as their gestures), pranks and other traditions of a radio station, and a host of other subjects limited only by students' imagination or instructors' guidelines. (Most folklore field collector's guides brim over with similar suggestions.)

Many fine topics for research papers do not require fieldwork. If your university has a folklore archive, you may be able to select one unit of its material for analysis and include recommendations in your paper for better arrangement of the section and published references that can be used for comparative annotation of the archival materials. A local historical society may have documentary or pictorial materials you can study, such as old diaries and family histories or photo albums showing pioneer dress, housing, and work customs. There are many potentially valuable bibliographic projects to be done, including an annotated bibliography of articles on using folklore in teaching, a compilation of folk speech in sports taken from a run of some magazine such as *Ski* or *Field and Stream,* and a list of articles discussing Western folklore that have been published over the course of five years in a series like *Frontier Times* or *Arizona Highways.*

Once you have an idea for a research paper, or at least a general subject area, you should talk it over with your instructor before getting involved in the actual gathering of sources. It may be that someone else has already done a similar project, and the instructor can redirect you to another aspect of it or to a more promising topic. (If you had wanted to write on the primacy of sight data as expressed in our folk sayings, for example, he or she could probably tell you that Alan Dundes has already written about that in "Seeing Is Believing," *Natural History*, 81 [May 1972], 8–12, 86–87. But how about the sense of hearing, as in "That ain't the way I heard it" or "In one ear and out the other"?) Further, your instructor is the only one who can tell you with authority how a subject might best be related to the particular course you are taking and what standards will be expected in coverage and documentation.

The whole process of selecting a general topic for your research, which can take from a few hours to a few days, should not require any thorough bibliographic search, although you may have to try out your library's resources on a few prospective subjects. You are ready to get seriously involved in the library (or in the field, as the case may be) only when you have in hand a specific topic that has been given preliminary approval by your instructor, and one that is preferably expressed in the form of a clear, concise question.

As you now prepare to do your research, you should be asking yourself a question something like one of these: "Do bumper stickers qualify as folklore?" or "How do people begin acquiring their attitudes toward different races through the folk rhymes of babyhood and early childhood?" or "What elements of folklore are there in Thomas Dekker's *The Shoemaker's Holiday* (1598)?" or "What are the folk traditions of shoe salesmen?" or "How do the Greeks of Price, Utah, celebrate Easter?" or "How much folklore has Ann Landers transmitted or dispelled in her columns of the past year?" or "Is Paul Bunyan dead or alive in current elementary school teaching aids?" or "Are Girl Scouts a folk group and are their camp songs folksongs?" or "Can 'formulaic-composition' theories explain the style of the 'confessions' of Weight Watchers or Alcoholics Anonymous?" or "What 'types' would a contextual or behavioral definition of 'folklore' seem to create or eliminate?" or "What are the arguments for and against retaining the term 'folklore' to refer to a scholarly field of study?" or "Has anyone written anything about the folklore of the small-town, old-time general store?"

Questions like these abound in folklore, and any good college library will have materials bearing in some way on them and on many more. Having selected your general topic and having phrased a preliminary question for research, you are ready to go to the library and prepare a working bibliography, thus getting into the real business of your research.

PREPARING A WORKING BIBLIOGRAPHY

Whether your subject requires research in book, or in the field, your first stop should be the college library. Even if your main goal is to collect living folklore, you need an idea of what to collect, how to collect it, and what has been published in the field. Besides, the general argument for analyzing your subject as folklore needs to be established on the firm basis of scholarly findings and opinions.

If you start your search for published material bearing on your subject by looking it up in the library card catalogue, or by trying to find a concise encyclopedia article on it, or by heading for what you hope is the appropriate section of the stacks, you will get nowhere fast. These may sound like the right and the easy ways to proceed, but they are not. You may only be led to conclude, probably incorrectly, that "no one has written *anything* about this subject, and the whole thing is hopeless." (Even if no one has written on the subject, the situation is not hopeless; you can write something on it.)

The *right* way to begin is with the information and advice contained in this guide, particularly with the bibliographies and reference works it identifies. In the process of checking such basic sources as the *Southern Folklore Quarterly* annual bibliography, Haywood's *Bibliography,* the Funk & Wagnalls *Standard Dictionary,* and the indexes to the *Journal of American Folklore, Folklore,* and other scholarly periodicals, you can also test out the immediate usefulness of the library catalogue numbers cited here. Likely you will discover that some of the given Library of Congress numbers will match those in your library exactly, and you can go directly to the shelves and find these books; other numbers will be a bit different, and you will need to pencil-in changes in your copy of the guide as you discover them. (*Pencil,* because you may be working in another library someday.) If your library uses the Dewey Decimal system, you will need to look up all the call numbers you need.

You need not ask a librarian for help until you have personally checked a particular author and title in the card catalogue, but if you fail to locate a catalogued work, don't be hesitant to ask for assistance. You should soon begin to become acquainted with the layout of your own library and some of its idiosyncrasies, such as where the reference works are shelved, which periodicals it subscribes to, how completely subjects are indexed in the card catalogue, and whether most basic folklore books are placed in one designated category ("GR" for LC, "398" for Dewey) or scattered in different categories, such as literature, music, and anthropology. It is easier to browse through some libraries than others when it comes to folklore.

If you are writing in a particular genre of folklore, be sure to read the appropriate chapters in the latest survey works and textbooks available to you. Take down references from their bibliographies to add to those given in this guide. Also, consult the standard indexes and editions of folklore genres. If you are concerned with a current folklore topic (such as folk traditions of Watergate or of drug addiction), be sure to locate the current unbound issues of the folklore periodicals to see what has been published lately.

Right from the start you must decide whether you are going to gather bibliographic references on slips or cards. Slips are cheaper (you can cut them up yourself), but cards are sturdier; in either case, you will do well to select a standard size such as three-by-five or four-by-six inches, which will fit a card-file drawer or envelope well and tuck easily into pocket or purse. Keep all your references on individual slips or cards—*never* more than one item per slip. Then you can easily sort them in different ways, discard the items you do not need in the end, and type your footnotes and bibliography directly from the organized slips.

Your first written record of a published reference source should contain all the information you may later need in order to cite it correctly: author, full title, and the facts of publication. It is also a good idea to enter your library's catalogue number in the front upper left-hand corner of the card or slip and to write your own brief general summary or evaluation of the work on the back (possibly a capsule table of contents of a book or a paraphrase of the main argument of an article).

Your reference card on a book might look like this:

```
NA7206              C.A. Weslager
W4
                    The Log Cabin in America from Pioneer
                    Days to the Present

                    New Brunswick, N.J.: Rutgers Univ. Press

                    1969
```

For an essay in a journal, the card might look like this:

```
David Evans

"Techniques of Blues Composition among Black Folksingers"

Journal of American Folklore, 87 (1974), 240-249
```

Notice that in these examples, as in proper footnote and bibliography form, the title of an *article* is in quotation marks and the title of a *book or journal* is underlined. Some internal punctuation may be omitted at this point since its final form will vary depending upon where and how in the paper the reference is used. For an entry on a journal, the volume number precedes the date, the page numbers follow it; both are in Arabic numerals. If there are multiple authors of a work, or if it is a later edition, a translation, part of a series, or has any other special features, take *all* this information down on your original card so that you will not have to go back to the source later on or, even worse, so you will not cite that work incorrectly in your paper.

At this stage of a research project, it is a good idea to keep careful track of *what* you have checked in *which* sources. For example, you may remember later that you checked Haywood's *Bibliography,* looking up "Blues" and "Spirituals." But did you also check for entries on "Toasties," "Dozens," and "Sounding" to complete your search for references on black oral-traditional genres? Often you do not really know until later in the project just what headings to use in a catalogue, bibliography, or index; if you fail to keep some such personal records, you may have to retrace your early steps.

Another time-saving device is to make a Xerox copy of the bibliography from some comprehensive recent scholarly work and then use this as a check list for your library search. For example, if you were hunting for published variants of a particular folksong, you might work from a copy of the bibliography in D. K. Wilgus's *Anglo-American Folksong Scholarship Since 1898,* checking off collections of texts as they are located and scanned. At the same time you would amend Wilgus's references to match the particular editions of the works available in your own library. Then bibliography cards for the sources that prove usable can be written up later from these annotated Xeroxed sheets. Following this procedure you also need to notice the cutoff date for items in the published bibliography so that you can look further for works to bring the material up to date.

Often the very best bibliographic guide is the most recent available documented study in the same field. One can then work backward through its footnotes and other references to the baseline studies in that subject.

A few hours of efficient labor in a good library should give you a fair idea of the potential of your subject. If you have collected more than a few dozen truly relevant sources, possibly the topic is still too broad and you need to revise it before you carry on. If you discover a source that seems to do exactly what you had set out to do, study it carefully to see if you can contribute some new materials or a personal point of view on the subject. If nothing at all seems to turn up, stop and consider whether instead of searching for studies of your particular narrow subject (i.e., bumper stickers, pool hustlers' tricks, skiers' jargon) you need to direct your attention to more general subjects like folklore of the automobile, gambling, sports, or some related genre (bumper stickers—graffiti? skiers— mountain climbers?). If you get into a complete muddle, have another talk with your instructor.

With your working bibliography shaping up as a thickening packet of reference slips, you are ready to sort them out in a rough preliminary fashion. Possibly they could be grouped as bibliographic sources, historical surveys, editions, studies (in chronological order), theoretical works, and miscellaneous (there is always a miscellaneous category at this stage). Of course, you will find other sources as you proceed, and not all your original finds will turn out to be useful in the end, but at this stage you should be getting into the material itself in order to take the notes that will eventually be employed in the writing of the paper.

GATHERING INFORMATION

Since the kinds of data needed for different folklore research projects vary a great deal in source and type, it is impossible to give detailed instructions here for all varieties of information gathering that a folklorist may have to engage in. However, with a few general hints, and using resources suggested in this guide, the student can be prepared for most contingencies.

Field collecting and tape transcription, especially of musical folklore, are complex subjects in themselves about which much useful advice has been published. It is possible, however, to collect oral folklore verbatim in the field by means of handwritten notes; many folklorists have done it, and most informants will adjust their rate of speech to accommodate a collector's speed. Handwritten collecting has the advantage of producing immediately usable textual material; sound recordings must still be transcribed before analysis.

Whether using notebook or tape recorder, the field collector probably will want to keep track of contextual and background information such as gestures, facial expressions, where the item was learned, audience response, and any variations that are known. Some kinds of oral folklore such as proverbs and riddles would seldom be recorded on tape, since they usually occur sporadically and unpredictably in conversation and are short enough to be quickly jotted down. But again, contextual information, such as the application to life situations of proverbs, or whether riddles are solved, should be noted.

When a collector uses a tape recorder, he or she must be sure to write the subject, date, and tape speed both on the tape box and reel (on a piece of adhesive tape or a special white leader strip). It is also advisable to "caption" the beginning of each recording session with an oral announcement of the same information.

Before a tape is transcribed it is useful to make an index of the general subjects contained on it, keying this to the length-counter on the recorder. (Not all machines line up the same, by the way.) For a folklore archive the entire tape would be transcribed, but for a limited research project, possibly only the particular texts or discussions being studied would need to be. In either method, of course, the transcription should be made letter-perfect from the recording. (This is a difficult job, but a foot control and earphones on the recorder can make it a little easier.)

Field interviews may be closely directed by the collector only toward topics he or she is interested in. The collector may want to employ questionnaires to insure that all informants are quizzed for the same range of data. Or the folklorist may prefer to let the speakers ramble on, hoping they will touch on related matters of interest to the study. Some fieldworkers prefer an initial free discussion with an informant, followed by a recorded interview centering on the notes taken on the first instance. This approach has the virtue of yielding recordings that stick to the point, although there is also danger of losing context and a natural style in the process. For some topics a researcher may simply be collecting "on the fly," that is, keeping a notebook always at hand to jot down the kind of folk tradition relevant to the research whenever he or she happens to encounter it.

Fieldwork in folklife obviously involves a student in a whole new set of concerns such as photography, drawing, mapping, measuring, and presentation of information on artifacts or behavior in the written report. Gestures, for example, could be described and photographed successfully, but what about string figures or children's games? Would your instructor accept a slide lecture on folk toys for the class in lieu of illustrations in the report? How many photos, sketches, or measurements are necessary to describe a log cabin completely and clearly?

Material found in folklore archives should be identified just as closely as that from one's own fieldwork—by source, date, place, and situation (insofar as these are known). The archival identification or classification terms or numbers should also be noted for the record.

By whatever means one collects folk material of whatever kind, the student may eventually want to transfer bits of the information to separate slips or cards that can be labeled by subject and sorted into different groupings. An alternate way to handle this matter is to work out an organizational scheme and then add marginal notes to the collected material using different colors of ink or pencil.

Probably much of one's material for a college research paper in folklore will come not from fieldwork or archives but from the same source as for any other term paper—published works found in the library. The techniques for taking notes from publications are pretty much the same in any field: each single idea or piece of information goes on a separate labeled slip or card, and careful track must be kept of the exact source and page referred to.

Before actually taking any serious notes from books or essays it is a good idea to read the whole work or the relevant portions of it through closely, jotting down brief topics of potential use in the paper along with their page references. The actual notes that are taken based on this scratch list will fall into three general categories —summary, paraphrase, and direct quotation—and each kind of note has its particular usefulness.

An efficient way to keep tabs on notes is to head each slip (four-by-six inches is a popular size) with the author's name, a short-title reference to the work (only if you are citing more than one item by the same author), the subject of the note, and the pages cited. Thus, a *summary* note on a chapter in Edward D. Ives's book *Larry Gorman: The Man Who Made the Songs* (when other works by Ives will also be cited) might look like this:

```
Ives, Gorman              Ch. XI "The Satirical Song Tradition"
                          pp. 167-179


     Ives finds a tradition of songs that humorously criticize
particular local subjects to be widespread in Britain, Canada,
and the United States, particularly dealing with agriculture,
mining, lumbering, and the sea.  There were many other
people in Larry Gorman's region who were known for composing
the same kinds of satirical songs that he did.  Four full examples
(three with music) and a number of fragments are quoted.
```

Such a note, which mainly serves to encapsulate a viewpoint or a
set of findings, might be recorded on the back of the bibliographic
slip or card for the book if that is more convenient.

Direct quotations taken down as notes should be literally accurate,
as printed, including errors (if any). The reader's omissions should
be indicated by ellipses marks (three spaced periods). The whole
passage is enclosed in quotation marks:

```
Ives, Gorman              Three Aspects of Folk Tradition
                          p. 168


     "Folk tradition can be thought of as having three aspects:
the creative, the prescriptive, and the conservative.  For the
first, the question is, was there a tradition of making up songs?
For the second, once a man decided to make up a song, did
his culture provide him with a stock of formulae upon which he
was not only able but expected to draw?  For the third, once a
song had been created, how far might it spread and how long might
it last in oral tradition?... The three aspects can exist in
different combinations of strengths, not only in different areas
but also for different genres within any given area."
```

A *paraphrase* restates a general idea of the author *in the note-taker's own words;* if any exact wording is included, quotation marks are necessary. A paraphrase is the first step between finding a usable idea in a published source and incorporating it into the structure and style of one's own study. Of course, any direct quotations incorporated in a paraphrase must be placed in quotation marks, and omissions must be indicated. Here is an example:

```
Ives, Gorman          The Prescriptive Tradition in Satire
                      pp. 168-169


     Of the three aspects Ives describes--creative, pre-
scriptive, and conservative--he finds the first to be of primary
concern.  Evidence is lacking for "more than hazy general-
izations about the prescriptive tradition in /169/ satire...."
There must, however, be some kinds of formula phraseology
that belong to traditional satirical songs, since we cannot
always tell "from purely stylistic evidence" which satirical
songs Gorman composed.  (That is, since he was writing in
an established folk tradition, some of his individuality was sup-
pressed.)
```

Notice that the exact page break in the passage is indicated.

As essential as careful note taking is for good research, there is definite danger of taking too many irrelevant notes, for you may later flounder in a sea of information as you try to write the paper. Only experience can tell you how many notes to take. Clearly refining the scope of your project at the outset will help to determine what notes you need, and obviously it is far better to take too many than too few notes. A rule of thumb might be never to quote when paraphrase will do, and to confine the noting of specific facts to just the actual fact and not the style in which it is set forth.

Again, as in compiling a working bibliography, Xerox copying facilitates some shortcuts for the modern library researcher. Often a few relevant pages of a publication may most conveniently be duplicated as a whole and the needed information underlined and noted in the margin, possibly using different colors for different subtopics. Using this method the identifying data on the source are written directly on the top of the Xeroxed pages. Or, if field-collected texts are being annotated, copies could be made of each item on a separate sheet and the sources of published variants listed below in an abbreviated form. (In both cases, a bibliography slip is prepared for each published source, as usual.)

If all locating of information and taking of notes has been done systematically by a method such as described here, the student should be able to sit down some quiet evening, with all the data neatly arranged before him or her, and fairly smoothly outline and write the paper.

WRITING THE PAPER

Each kind of folklore project and possibly even each individual researcher may require a somewhat different style of presentation of the results of research. In dealing with certain topics, some people can write logically and lucidly by working directly from the sorted note and bibliography slips, just checking off or turning over each slip as it is used. I know one folklorist whose habit of composition is to stack up all around his study the publications from which he intends to quote—each one dangling its paper bookmarks—and then to transfer the books and journals from one side of his desk to the other as they are cited in the paper.

Most student writers, however, should do more preliminary planning than this before beginning to write the first draft of a paper. Whenever the researcher has done the work well and kept the thesis firmly in mind as he or she gathered information to support it, the orderly logic of the written presentation should come easily to mind. The labels on the note slips should fall into place in a clear outline of the paper's argument, and the bibliographic references should all be complete and ready to insert as needed. Finding himself or herself in this happy situation, all the writer might need to do is reread the notes one more time, draw up a list of topics and subtopics, and then commence writing.

To outline or not to outline? Some instructors require outlines, few students like them, and many good papers have been written without them. If you do outline your subject before writing the paper (and probably most beginning writers should), be aware that the outline represents in a skeletal way the formal logical structure of your argument leading up to a valid conclusion. Therefore, the outline itself must be logical, with its parts in coherent order, no single divisions of topics, and all headings in parallel grammatical form. The conventional form of an outline looks like the following:

I.
  A.
    1.
    2.
  B.
II.
  A.
  B.
  C.
    1.
    2.
III.
  (And so forth)

A sentence outline—with each topic expressed as an original grammatically complete sentence—takes longer to compose than an outline made up of one- or two-word subtopics, but it has the advantage of helping to insure that the paper is not just a paste-up of others' words. Such an outline is also helpful to the sluggish writer, since once the sentences have been composed many can be reused as topic sentences in the paper itself. This gives the student something to start on when facing the intimidating glare of blank pages.

It is this writer's personal opinion that outlining per se has no value except insofar as it helps a writer to write. If a paper is not clear without a prefatory outline, then an outline will not help it. If a student can write a logical paper from a set of rough notes and topics (I can), so be it. Outlining is a skill, like typing or speed reading, that may help you a good deal, or it may simply not be your thing. In any case, I have never been convinced of the usefulness of headings in outlines such as "Introduction" and "Conclusion," for they always lead to such dreadful phrases as "By way of introduction to our topic, let us . . ." and "Therefore, in conclusion, it may be said that . . ."

Many subjects in folklore research pose special problems in format that should be solved before the actual writing of the paper begins. For example, if there are collected texts of folk material involved, should all of these be quoted and discussed in the body of the paper, or should some be gathered in an appendix? How should illustrations be included? (Generally, these are inserted as close as possible to where they are discussed in the paper, then numbered in sequence and captioned concisely.) A collecting project may need to have a list of informants attached, possibly keyed to abbreviations —Informant A, B, C, and so on—used in the body of the paper. If a tape recording accompanies the paper, a tape index is also needed to cue the reader.

With the notes organized, the order of subjects decided on, and the outline (if any) prepared, the writer is at last ready to write. Here, of course, enters the *big* problem—how to get started. Few situations in life are so conducive to chronic procrastination and stomach ache than the unnatural act of putting one's thoughts down on paper in some coherent fashion.

Hemingway used to stop a writing session only when he had in mind the idea or wording for what would come next; thus, once he started, he never had to sit down with a blank mind. Fine so far, but how do you get started in the first place? Here an old journalist's slogan applies: "Don't get it right, get it written." In other words, you can always rewrite and improve the style of what you have put on paper, but until you get *something* down you have nothing even to work on. Get it written. Start writing. Put your ideas down in any fashion. No matter if your sentences are awkward at first; take comfort that at least you have begun.

What you want to achieve as you write this report is not a gem of "creative" composition, but only a clear, direct, and interesting account of your research and your findings. Do this without verbal frills, rhetorical fireworks, or a self-consciously folksy style. Prefer the active voice to the passive, the concrete term to the abstract. Address yourself to an intelligent but nonspecialized reader, bearing in mind that the paper is not a letter to your teacher. Use the technical language of your subject ("motif," "blues ballad," "dovetail corner notching," etc.) but don't assume anything; define your terms. As you write, keep in mind whether you are reporting the *record* of your research or the *product* of it. (Possibly you should have discussed this point with your instructor in advance, and certainly you should have decided it when outlining the paper.) In the former kind of paper you will retrace what you have done in chronological order; in the latter you will structure the paper around the order of ideas that develops your thesis to the point of a conclusion.

The basic unit of your writing is the paragraph—the unified, coherent building block of the whole essay. Each paragraph should be a distinct self-contained portion of the whole, following logically from the one before and leading logically to the next. Although some paragraphs are essentially transitional, introductory, conclusive, recapitulative, or the like, most paragraphs advance the ideas in the paper by means of topic and development. Often this takes the form of a topic sentence followed by several sentences of example, development, expansion, chronology, argument, explanation of a process, and the like. Other paragraphs begin with the development and lead up to a sentence of conclusion.

You should strive for some rhythm and variety in your sentences, although the straight subject-verb-object pattern will serve to get things down, and you can revise the style later. The same holds for word choice: get it written now, and revise later.

Some writers, especially those who feel insecure about their research or composition skills, tend to quote too much. Put the bulk of the discussion into your own words, quoting and paraphrasing selectively only to support your argument and develop your topic. Whenever you quote, summarize, or paraphrase from another's work, you must credit the source with a footnote or an attribution in the body of the paper. To do anything else is plagiarism or, in blunt language, stealing.

The deliberate plagiarist, like the false-hearted lover in the folksong, is "worse than a thief," because he or she lifts not merely another's goods but also that person's very thought and words. Any experienced instructor can detect a plagiarist in folklore research, because the field is still small enough to have only a relatively few published authorities on any subject worth stealing from; also, good instructors will know their students' styles and capabilities rather well by the end of a semester. Deliberate plagiarists deserve what they get, and they all get it sooner or later. Enough about that unsavory minority.

Accidental plagiarism is much more common, regrettable, and avoidable. Students sometimes unwittingly steal material for research papers because of carelessness in the original taking of notes or because exact details of wording and reference get lost in the shuffle of handling the notes from day to day. The whole problem can be avoided by forcing yourself to be systematic and careful every step of the way; when you copy something, copy it correctly and use quotation marks. When you paraphrase, be aware that merely altering some words in a sentence does not make that sentence either your own idea or your own phraseology.

Students need to be especially careful of incorporating material into their writing that was taken down in classroom lectures. Often your teacher may be quoting or paraphrasing other authorities, but when you look at such words in your notebook, you may have forgotten to whom they were attributed in class. If you want to quote lecture material, check back with your instructor for the source reference; if it was wholly the instructor's own words and ideas, get the quotation verified and credit it properly in the paper.

Overdocumentation is the frequent result of a student's concern not to plagiarize. If every little scrap of material in your paper is being footnoted at the rate of a note every few lines, then you are not *writing* a paper, you are just compiling it. You may need to get a little further from your notes and start again. Bear in mind that well-known factual information (such as the year the word "folklore" was coined) need not be footnoted.

For each footnote that you will need, insert raised numbers in sequence through the whole paper at the end of every quoted or paraphrased section and following the punctuation. It is not necessary to type the footnotes as the paper is being written nor to leave space for them at the bottom of pages, for they go on a separate sheet at the end. The format for these references is provided in the next section.

It is advisable to compose a rough draft of the complete paper before agonizing over the precise style and form of its separate parts. This both creates a sense of accomplishment and gives you the chance to see the whole project before you and to judge how alterations in one part may affect the rest. Every draft—whether type-written or handwritten—should be put on one side of the page only, with generous margins on all four sides.

Revision and proofreading are important but often neglected stages in preparing a research paper, for this is when you produce the actual paper that the instructor will read. Much of the real writing takes place then. This is the time when most writers work out beginnings, endings, and transitions. Now comes the chance to cut out the deadwood in your style, remove unnecessary repetitions, link short related sentences by using conjunctions or semicolons, and improve your choice of examples and facts to support the generalizations.

One needs plenty of time to revise well; it is tiring and slow work. The best procedure is to have several complete readings and revisions before typing the final paper. Allow time, if you can, to put the paper aside for a day or so and then return for a fresh look. It is also advisable to read through the paper for a different specific matter each time—for transitions, for the logical order of ideas, for style, and for mechanics of punctuation, spelling, and syllabification.

When the final paper has been typed, it must be proofread, for the errors that remain are your own, not the typewriter's. Professional proofreaders follow the practice of rereading any sentence entirely in which they have found an error, and then reading the whole section through one more time. You shouldn't have wasted much time and effort when you were writing the paper looking up words in a dictionary, but you are foolish now if you don't check yourself on doubtful spellings as you proofread.

FOOTNOTES AND BIBLIOGRAPHY

Footnotes should cause you no distress. Their chief use is simply to cite the pages in works from which direct quotations were taken or to identify the sources of any ideas that were borrowed, whether as paraphrase or summary. Whenever possible without interrupting the flow of ideas in a paper, part of the source information (such as the author's name) should be incorporated directly into the body of the paper. (Information given there should not be repeated in a footnote.) Although occasionally a footnote may include extra explanatory information about a source, there is seldom justification for inserting any material beyond source information in footnotes. If an idea or fact is relevant to the paper, it belongs in the text.

Standard footnote form nowadays is clear and logical, based on this sequence of information: author, title, facts of publication, page, all separated by commas. All the information needed for your footnotes is on your bibliography slips or cards, and you need merely to sort them into the correct order for the paper, select the required facts, and punctuate the notes properly. There is no need to use the esoteric Latin abbreviations once so beloved of scholars.

The form of documentation described here is that presented in *The MLA Style Sheet,* 2nd ed., which is available in many university bookstores or directly by mail at a small charge from the Publications Center, Modern Language Association, 62 Fifth Avenue, New York, N.Y. 10011. This concise pamphlet gives detailed sensible advice on the writing and documenting of research that has become the standard practice of most scholarly presses and journals in the humanities.

In all footnotes the author's name in normal order comes first, followed by a comma. Titles of books are underlined, as are the names of periodicals; titles of chapters in books (if cited) and of essays are enclosed in quotation marks. The publication information for a book (place, colon, publisher, comma, date) is put within parentheses, as is the year of publication of a journal. No punctuation directly precedes parentheses. The volume number of a journal precedes the date, and the page reference follows the date; both are always in Arabic numerals. A book reference needs "p." for "page" or "pp." for "pages," but a journal reference does not.

All footnotes are gathered at the end of the research paper starting on a separate sheet headed "Notes." Footnotes are double-spaced throughout. Every footnote is indented five spaces (like a paragraph) and ends with a period (like a sentence). Each footnote number is typed slightly above the line and followed only by one blank space before the text of the note itself.

The following examples illustrate basic footnote forms and a few of the common variations:

1. A book with a single author.

   [1] A. L. Lloyd, *Folk Song in England* (New York: International Publishers, 1967), p. 119.

2. A book with two or more authors.

   [2] John T. Flanagan and Arthur Palmer Hudson, eds., *Folklore in American Literature* (Evanston, Ill.: Row, Peterson, 1958), pp. 51–52.

3. A work in several volumes.

   [3] Richard M. Dorson, ed., *Peasant Customs and Savage Myths: Selections from the British Folklorists* (Chicago: University of Chicago Press, 1968), I, 67–68. [The Roman numeral stands for volume I, and then the "p." for "page" can be omitted.]

   [4] Newman Ivey White, gen. ed., *The Frank C. Brown Collection of North Carolina Folklore*, I (Durham, N.C.: Duke University Press, 1952), 87. [The difference in placing the volume number reflects the fact that Dorson's volumes were published the same year, whereas the seven volumes of White's work appeared in different years.]

4. A later edition or modern reprint of a book.

   [5] George Webbe Dasent, *Popular Tales from the Norse*, 3rd ed. (Edinburgh: David Douglas, 1888), p. 436. [A later edition may be revised or contain new material.]

   [6] Henry Carrington Bolton, *The Counting-Out Rhymes of Children* (1888; rpt. Detroit: Singing Tree Press, 1969), p. 69. [This is a reprint of the book originally published in 1888.]

5. An essay in a collection.

   [7] Edith Fowke, "A Sampling of Bawdy Ballads from Ontario," in *Folklore and Society: Essays in Honor of Benj. A. Botkin*, ed. Bruce Jackson (Hatboro, Pa.: Folklore Associates, 1966), p. 50.

6. An article in a scholarly journal.

   [8] Mary and Herbert Knapp, "Tradition and Change in American Playground Language," *Journal of American Folklore*, 86 (1973), 137.

7. An article in a popular periodical.

   [9] Carroll Calkins and Alan Lomax, "Getting to Know Folk Music," *House Beautiful*, April 1960, pp. 140–141. [Popular periodicals, unlike scholarly ones, are paged separately in each issue instead of by the entire year, and although they may have a volume number, it generally makes more sense to cite both the month and year of publication. Since no volume number is given, "p." or "pp." is needed with the page number(s).]

8. A book review in a journal.

[10] John E. Keller, rev. of *They Sang for Horses: The Impact of the Horse on Navajo and Apache Folklore* by LaVerne Harrell Clark, *Southern Folklore Quarterly*, 31 (1967), 75.

Most of the other possible complications in footnote form can be solved by the application of good common sense. For example, if the author of a work is not given, then begin the note with the title. Or, if a quotation occurs within an essay title, then use double quotes around the whole title and single quotes internally. *The MLA Style Sheet* and your instructor are rich mines of information on such interesting matters as these.

Once a reference has been fully cited in a footnote, subsequent references to the same book or essay should be put in the shortest possible form that is perfectly clear. Generally in a research paper this will be the author's last name plus the page reference; a subsequent reference to Roger L. Welsch's book *Shingling the Fog and Other Plains Lies* could be cited simply as:

[11] Welsch, p. 12.

Or, if more than one work by Welsch has been cited, a shortened form of the appropriate title is also needed, as here in this alternate form of the note:

[11] Welsch, *Lies,* p. 16.

These two forms are used for all subsequent references to the same book, even when more than one footnote in succession refers to the same source.

Remember that the rule given earlier about source information in the text of the paper also applies here: if you included it in the text, you don't need it again in the footnote. Some writers even put simple page references parenthetically in the text rather than cluttering their writing with many short footnotes.

A full bibliography of all sources consulted for a research paper should be placed after the footnotes beginning on a separate sheet headed "Select Bibliography" or "List of Works Consulted." In a short project if every source consulted was quoted and cited in the paper, a separate bibliography may not be needed, although an instructor may want to require one in order to call attention to the small differences in their standard form as compared to footnotes.

The bibliography is typed double-spaced with all works arranged alphabetically according to authors' last names. This time the authors' names are given in reverse order. There are no numbers for bibliography items, and each one begins flush left on the page with subsequent lines indented. The main parts of each entry are now separated by periods rather than commas. Facts of publication for books are no longer enclosed in parentheses, and the inclusive page numbers for chapters in books and articles in periodicals must be given. Most of these aspects of bibliographic form are illustrated in the model research paper that follows and need not be demonstrated separately here.

MODEL RESEARCH PAPER

The following example of a short research paper in folklore illustrates one commonly accepted form of beginning student research, an annotated collection of folk material from the student's own background region. All the personal names in the paper are actual; they are used here with the permission of the persons quoted.

Three Southern Utah Storytellers

Vanna Hunter
English 517
5 March 1975

Introduction

I was born and raised in Cedar City,
Utah, a community of some 9,000 people lying
260 miles south of Salt Lake City in Iron
County. My father was a farmer and a sheepman,
as was his father before him, and my mother's
father was a stockman and dairyman. My life
has been colored by these occupations and
especially by the land of southern Utah; this
land and its people seemed a natural source for
my folklore project.

The oral folklore herein was collected
with the help of my mother, Odessa Ford Hunter,
using a borrowed cassette tape recorder and
visiting some of her friends in mid January 1975.
We tried to get a good cross section of the oral
narrative tradition of the area. After transcribing
the tapes, I organized the stories to best
represent the repertoires of my three chief
informants into three general categories: local
history, local character tales, and tall tales.
I have attempted to annotate only the last section
thoroughly with variants found in published
collections. The titles to the stories are my
own.

Most major settlements in southwestern
Utah were made in the 1850s and 1860s by Mormon
pioneers sent south by Brigham Young to establish
towns. These people were mainly of British
extraction with some Swedes and Germans. The
Cedar City area was initially settled because of
the iron deposits to the west, while the Hurricane
and St. George areas were established to produce
cotton and sorghum. Although these industries
were developed, farming and livestock raising
soon became the predominant vocations. As Lehi
Jones says, "... sheep and cattle were the only
things that they could walk in and then walk out
to market."

The pioneers had some difficulty adjusting
to the area. Most of them had come from amply
watered countries in Europe or from the eastern
United States and found themselves suddenly faced
with a very dry and often harsh land. Growing up
in "Cedar," as we natives call our city, I have
seen the temperature vary from over 100 degrees in
the summer to as much as 30 degrees below zero in
the winter. The wind seems to blow constantly
and at times with great force. Irrigation is
required for any kind of farming.

The livestock industry in the area soon

developed a general pattern of adaptation to these conditions. During the winter months sheep and cattle were kept out on the "range," that is, on the desert areas of southwestern Utah, northern Arizona (the "Arizona strip"), and eastern Nevada. There the livestock grazed on what browse and grass there was. Often water had to be hauled to the stock, and there were herders who stayed with them at a camp. Then, in May or June, depending on the weather, the livestock were driven to summer range on "the mountain." This general term refers to a large territory, but is well understood by anyone who has had any experience in the local livestock industry. "The mountain" includes all of the area east and south of Cedar City in what is now the Dixie National Forest and the Kolob Terrace. The topography here is quite alpine and generally provides good feed throughout the summer months and into September and October. At this time the livestock were driven back out to the winter range.

My three major informants who are quoted in this paper are in their seventies or eighties and have had long and close association with the area and its typical industries. In their folk narratives we can easily see how the natural

environment in southern Utah, the people's
unfamiliarity with it, and their responses to
living and working there have influenced the oral
traditions.

Lehi Jones--Local History Stories

Lehi Jones is a name that I have grown up
with, a local livestock man who has also been
involved in several other businesses. I remember
him working a great deal with my father. He is
eighty-four years old, but you wouldn't guess it,
for he still goes out to his farm and puts in a
full day's work. He is tall and slender with white
hair, a wiry, rugged, down-to-earth, practical,
conservative, and very friendly man. A few years
back he made a stir in the community when he refused
to accept Social Security payments; when they sent
his check to him, he sent it back.

As might be expected, Lehi Jones's stories
deal with the livestock business. The following
three incidents as he tells them are rather humorous
and quite representative of local history traditions.
The first deals with the early settlers' initiation
into the sheep business, and the last two with
pranks played by cowboys.

A Lesson in Sheepraising

This is Lehi Jones from Cedar City. I was asked about the sheep business in early days. Of course the sheep and cattle were brought here so the people could live. They had nothing to live on without something that would eat the grass and browse that was here when they come. So, sheep and cattle were the only things that they could walk in and then walk out to market when they developed. Well, anyway, the people that were here were from Sweden, and England, and Wales, and Scotland, and Germany; and they knew nothing about range animals and how to handle them. It's told that after they'd fed off the area close around Cedar City, they moved out into the other valley beyond Iron Springs and were grazing close around the water, of course, at first, and they'd moved up about four or five miles away from the water up to what is known as Desert Mound. They were trailing them back down to the water at Iron Springs whenever they needed to drink.

During one of the first winters they were in there it come a heavy snow, probably a foot and a half to two feet of snow. The herder who was handling the sheep--or herders, they had several men out with one little bunch to keep the coyotes and other varmints away from them--and they sent word in that the sheep were snowed in and they couldn't get them down to where they could get a drink and they were in bad shape. So, the call went out from the bishop,[1] or whoever else was in charge of the co-op sheep, for all the men they could get--everybody to go out and tromp trails from Iron Springs up to Desert Mound to make it so the sheep could walk down there and get a drink.

Well, of course they responded, and everybody that was able to, I guess maybe about five or six times more than they needed, come out and they worked all day tromping trails so they could get the sheep down to drink. They were real disgusted and discouraged when they got them down there. The sheep weren't interested in water; they'd had all the snow they wanted to. That was quite a lesson they learned, one of the first lessons they learned, about handling sheep.[2]

The Pot-on-the Head Prank[3]

This story about Iron Springs has to do with cattle
and things that went on in early days, about
gathering and handling cattle, marking and branding,
and sorting out the ones they wanted to sell and
bring into market or whatever. There was a little
rock house north of Iron Springs and that was the
general campground. They could camp inside
whenever it was stormy or cold. Most the time they
cooked outside, just outside, and had their beds
inside on the floor or wherever they could get them.
They had a lot of nonsense going on around these
campfires, like there is today where young fellows
are associated. They were cutting tricks on one
another, and among the things that went on somebody
took a big old iron kettle that is used to cook
stews and whatever when a good big pot of food is
needed, and went up behind one of the cowboys that
was sitting down there and pushed this pot, set
this pot, they thought it'd go on his head. Instead
of that it went down over his ears and down around
his neck, and when he went to shake it off it
wouldn't come off. And, of course, the fellow that
put it on was kind of alarmed that he couldn't get
this pot back off.

They did everything they knew how to get
it off. They went in every kind of imaginable
position to get this kettle off and finally in
desperation, they decided the only thing to do was
to have him lay his head on a block and hit the
kettle with a ax hard enough to break the kettle.
Of course, that would entail maybe damaging his
hearing with a ring like that going on. But anyway,
the man who was suffering with the pot on his head
decided he'd have to try something so in the process
of having him get his head down on a block where
somebody could hit it with an ax, it happened to get
in the same position as it was when it went on--the
pot slipped off very handily. And that relieved
the whole of the situation for all concerned, mainly
the fellow was relieved that put the pot on his
head in the first place.

Bull in the Bunkhouse

At this same location, north of Iron Springs at the

old Rock Camphouse they used to call it, it's told
that, apparently it must have been colder weather,
and everybody was inside after they'd eaten and got
through with the nonsense that went on at those
early campout roundup years. And everybody had
their bed--there must have been twelve to maybe
twenty men there--and they had their beds just
about covering the whole floor area of this camp,
and two or three or four fellows, they'd taking to
handling this wild yearling bull that they had in
the corral. They'd probably been thinking about it
all day--what they were going to do--because they
had to have him under control.

When everybody had quieted down they thought
it was about time that they were all in bed, why
two or four of these boys got this bull and took
him over and opened the door and pushed him into
the house. If you can think of a bull in a china
closet causing havoc, I imagine that you'd see these
fellows hanging from the side of the walls or
jumping wherever they could get to get out of the
road of this bull in the dark, you'd probably have
some idea of the confusion that went on. I don't
know that anybody lived to tell the story of how
they come out. But that's one of the pranks,
rather a wild story, but many of those went on in
early days.

Lanell Lunt--Local Character Anecdotes

Local character anecdotes are a kind of
extension of local history, but rather than dealing
with specific events, they are concerned with
particular local people and their amusing or
peculiar traits of character. These stories are
often humorous and generally do not spread beyond
the local area where the people are known, for you
must know the person (at least by reputation) to
truly appreciate the anecdote.

The local character anecdote is Lanell
Lunt's speciality. Not only does he have a good
sense of the humorous, but he is adept at mimicking
others. Because of this his stories cannot be
truly appreciated without hearing him tell them.
Mr. Lunt also makes use of a kind of technique of
misdirection, seeming to start out with one idea and
then changing his emphasis in the middle of the story.
One gets the impression that he is improvising a
tale rather than telling a well-rehearsed story like
Otto Fife's tall tales in the next section.

Lanell Lunt has been a businessman in
Cedar City. He is seventy-five years old and has
been active in church and community affairs. He is
of medium height and rather slight build. Each of
the stories quoted here has some bearing on the
predominant Mormon culture of the region, and the
strategy of each story is to lead up to a comic
statement by the character being described.

George Millet's Insurance

George Millet was an outstanding character in the
early history of Cedar City. He was a unique
character, sort of a visionary man, and they used
to have a lot of fun with him and he made a lot of
fun for the townspeople. On one occasion Bishop
E. M. Corry, who was selling insurance and also
worked in the bank, approached George in an attempt
to sell him some insurance. And, I would like to
relate to you in George's own words how the
conversation went. George related that, after much

persuasion, he decided to take the policy. And on
the next Fast Sunday he stood up in testimony
meeting[4] and said:

"My brothers and sisters, I'm here today as
a living testimony to you that insurance is of the
Devil. After much persuasion by Bishop Corry, I
consented to take out the life insurance policy. I
went home and asked the Lord to open up the way for
met to get the money to pay the premium, and to this
day my prayers have not been answered. The money was
never provided so that I could pay the premium,
therefore, I know that insurance is of the Devil!"

George Millet in the Movies

On another occasion when one of the movie companies
was filming "Brigham Young"--this was back in the
middle 1930s--they were filming out in the Iron
Springs Gap. There was a caravan of covered wagons
approaching the movie camera and also quite a number
of men on foot. The movie people used quite a
number of the local people here as extras. And, as
the caravan approached the movie camera, the
director, who was standing at a higher elevation,
could see someone that was walking that was not
dressed appropriately representing the mode of
dress that the pioneers wore. The director called
down to the cameraman and told him to "Get that man
out of there!" And he repeated it the second or third
time, "Get that man out of there!" As they
approached nearer to the camera, someone took George
bodily and put him in back of a wagon and as they
completed shooting this particular part of the film,
George walked up to the director and said: "I would
like you to know that I'm just as good a Latter-day
Saint as any man in that group!"

Oscar Larsen Risks One Eye

Oscar Larsen was another interesting character. As
a small boy he came to this country from Sweden.
Arriving in New York City he worked there for some
time with an uncle in a blacksmith shop. While
working in this blacksmith shop, a spark from the
anvil caused the loss of one eye. He came to Cedar
City where two of his boyhood friends, Albert
Lundale and Charlie Lundgren, were engaged in the
sheep business. At the age of fifty, Oscar was one

of Cedar City's more well-to-do citizens and a
director in the Bank of Southern Utah. Some years
ago the Las Vegas Chamber of Commerce hosted the
Cedar City Chamber of Commerce and among the group
was Oscar Larsen and William R. Palmer, who at that
time was president of the Cedar Stake.[5] President
Palmer had also lost one eye as a small boy. As
the group was shown around Las Vegas, they came to
the old "red light" district. As the driver of the
bus started down the street, Oscar turned to Will
and said: "Vell, vell, Vill. I vill risk one eye
if you vill!"[6]

The Phonograph Salesman

I grew up on a small farm about a mile west of
Cedar. As a young man one Christmas time I
accompanied my father into town where we went to
the Harry Leigh furniture store where father was
interested in buying a phonograph for the family
Christmas present. As we entered the store, Harry
Leigh greeted us and showed us around the store,
and father told him that he was interested in a
phonograph. And this is about the way the
conversation went:
     "Well, Will, I'm very happy to have you
come in and glad to know that you're interested in
a phonograph. Now, we have here several different
types but the one that I think is the best is the
Thomas A. Edison Machine. It's superb in tone and
quality and the workmanship of the cabinet is
unsurpassed by none. Now, if you'll have a seat
here for just a moment, I'll play you this record.
It's entitled 'In the Shade of the Old Apple Tree'
on the front side and 'I Wonder Who's Kissing Her
Now' on the back side."

Otto Fife--Tall Tales

Americans have an affinity for outrageous

lies, and tall tales, although originated in Europe,

have become a standard form of folk humor in the

United States. They are found throughout the land,

often the same story many times over with local
adaptations. They are an excellent example of the
transmission of folklore and of the styles of
regional alteration.

Otto Fife is a born tall-tale teller, spinning
one unbelievable story after another with great skill
and always a straight face. He is an institution in
Cedar City, about seventy-five years old, tall with
graying hair, a former sheriff of Iron County, and
an ardent outdoorsman who still does a great deal
of hiking and camping. Every tall tale he told me
can be found in variants from other parts of the
United States, but each one has been somehow adapted
to the southern Utah locale. Otto Fife tells his
stories in a flowing manner, rarely ending a sentence
but instead stringing them together with "and,"
"but," or some other conjunction.

Dust in the Face

I've had a lot of experience in this country. I
do a lot of hiking and traveling. For several
years I lived out at Beryl, out at the Escalante
Valley, and that was the windiest dustiest place I
had ever been.
    They were breaking up ground making farms
and one year we had wind there and dust flying and
the people sorta got used to it. And it was dry,
and one day it quit blowing and the dust settled
a little and the clouds came up and one fellow looked
up at the cloud half frightened--he didn't know
what it was--and a rain drop hit him in the face,

and he fainted, and we had to get a bucket of dust
to throw in his face to revive him.

Ernest W. Baughman has assigned this tale
the motif X1641.1*(a). and he reports two versions
from the Southwest.[7] Vance Randolph, for example,
collected it near Tahlequah, Oklahoma, told on a man
named Tom Burnside.[8] In a cowboy version a bucket
of sand is used to revive the man.[9] Among Otto
Fife's other stories concerning dry weather is this
traditional anecdote:

Praying for Rain

In the early days when the people were in there they
were very religious and they depended a lot on the
power of Deity to help them out. So, when it would
get pretty dry in there they would--in their Sunday
church--they'd pray for rain. This one day--they'd
had a long drought--the Bishop asked one of the
Elders to open the meeting on Sunday, and he says,
"Now, I want you to pray for rain." He says, "Our
livestock and our crops are suffering for the want
of moisture." The fellow looked at him, and he
says, "Well I'll do it, Bishop, but I don't believe
it will do a damn bit of good as long as the wind
is in the north."

As Mody Boatright described the same story, which was
"current in West Texas," it would do no good there
to pray with the wind in the west.[10]

The Hat in the Puddle

I was going there once and I saw a big mud puddle off

the side--a great big puddle--and there was a
beautiful cowboy hat lying on it. And I thought
the cowboy, it'd probably blown off and he was
scared to get it. So, I got a long stick and
reached over and hooked it, and when I got it
there was a fellow under it! He says, "Hey, put
that back!" And I said, "My goodness you're in
trouble, you'll have to have help to get out of
there won't you!" He says, "No, I'll make it.
I'm a-riding a darn good horse!"

The long and complicated history of this

tale (motif X1655.1.) in American folklore and

literature was traced by Jan Harold Brunvand.[11]

More recent versions have been collected on the

Great Plains[12] and in Maine.[13]

Hot Ice

I remember one winter out there it was awful cold.
My goodness! It would just freeze you if you got
out in it very long. We had a pan of boiling water
there and wanted to cool it, so I set it outside to
cool. It was so cold out there that it froze that
boiling water into ice so quickly that the ice was
still hot!

Baughman's index lists this tale as occurring

in oral tradition from the Eastern states to the Far

West and being included several times in the

popularized Paul Bunyan cycle; it is motif

X1622.3.3.1*. Ice freezes so rapidly (from water or

coffee) that it is still warm. Lowell Thomas

received one version from Pennsylvania, in which

the steaming hot water being carried by firemen to

a burning barn froze rapidly into warm ice, and in
his text from Alaska a ship's cook set a bucket of
boiling water outside the galley to cool and it
froze into hot ice.[14] Vance Randolph's variant from
Sulphur Springs, Arkansas, maintains that on a cold
day when a cabin door is left open briefly the
coffee on the stove will freeze into hot ice.[15] In
the Nebraska version it is a pitcher of water set
out to cool that freezes instantly.[16]

Too Hot for the Chickens

But the summers get pretty hot out there too. I
remember one summer it got so hot that the people
that had chickens there had to feed them cracked
ice to keep them from laying hard-boiled eggs.

While Baughman includes the general motif
of this tale, X1633. Lie: effects of heat on
animals, he has no specific references to chickens
and eggs. However, precisely this story was
published in the Nebraska Farmer for 1925 and
attributed to a man from Arizona.[17]

Wind Steals the Well

One fellow out there was quite perturbed. We had
a heavy wind and it blew his well out of his place
and blew it over into the neighbor's lot. Well,
before he could get over to get it the darn neighbor
had it all sawed up for postholes and he was using
'em around there then.

The blowing out of holes in the ground by the wind has one motif in Baughman (X1611.1.15.1*.), and sawing them up into short lengths for postholes has another (X1761.1.). There are numerous versions from all over the country involving both oil wells and water wells. J. Frank Dobie attributed his knowledge of the lie only to "the population of Texas,"[18] while John Lee Brooks identifies it as an exploit of Paul Bunyan's.[19] On the Great Plains sometimes postholes themselves are blown out of the ground, or rather the dirt around them is blown away; using sawn wells for new ones is said to be "a great deal better than buying his postholes from a mail-order house, as is so commonly done where the ground is too hard to dig them."[20] Otto Fife's version is somewhat different from the published texts in that the well itself is blown away and the man's neighbor, not the owner of the well, benefits.

These stories are but samples of the rich oral tradition of southern Utah, which takes many forms besides that of folk narratives. Last summer my mother and I visited a cousin of hers who was out herding sheep on the mountain. We found him at home in his one-room cabin baking bread in an old wood stove. As we walked with him through a meadow that was just swarming with grasshoppers, he remarked matter-of-factly, "We don't have a single grasshopper on the mountain ... they're all married and have large families."

Notes

[1] The bishop is the chief official and the spiritual leader of a Latter-day Saints "ward," or local congregation.

[2] The lesson they learned, of course, was that sheep will eat snow for the moisture they need to live.

[3] Pranks and practical jokes as a form of frontier humor are discussed in Mody C. Boatright's Folk Laughter on the American Frontier (New York: Macmillan, 1949). See also Stan Hoig, The Humor of the American Cowboy (Caldwell, Idaho: Caxton Press, 1958; paperback ed. New York: Signet 1960), pp. 18-21.

[4] The first Sunday of each month is "Fast Sunday" for the Latter-day Saints, and in place of regular speakers at church services members of the congregation are expected to "bear their testimonies" by relating experiences that have strengthened their faith in the church's teachings.

[5] The Latter-day Saints stake is a regional organizational unit consisting of several wards.

[6] Dialect humor of this sort is common in Utah; see, for example, "Danish Dialect Stories of the Mormon Church," in Richard M. Dorson, Buying the Wind:

Regional Folklore in the United States (Chicago:
University of Chicago Press, 1964), pp. 515-520.
A variant of the risk-one-eye story from Missouri
with references to others from Arkansas and
Pennsylvania appears in Mac E. Barrick, "Folktales
from the Institute at Duke," North Carolina
Folklore Journal, 23 (1975), 75-81.

[7]All motif references in this paper come from
Ernest W. Baughman, Type and Motif-Index of the
Folktales of England and North America, Indiana
University Folklore Series, No. 20 (The Hague,
The Netherlands: Mouton & Co., 1966).

[8]We Always Lie To Strangers: Tall Tales from the
Ozarks (New York: Columbia University Press, 1951),
p. 186.

[9]Hoig, pp. 37-38.

[10]Boatright, p. 135.

[11]"The Hat-in-Mud Tale" in The Sunny Slopes of
Long Ago, Publications of the Texas Folklore
Society, No. 33 (Dallas: Southern Methodist
University Press, 1966), pp. 100-109.

[12]Roger L. Welsch, Shingling the Fog and Other
Plains Lies (Chicago: Swallow Press, 1972), p. 50.

[13]C. Richard K. Lunt, "Jones Tracy, Tall-Tale Hero from Mount Desert Island," Northeast Folklore, 10 (1968), 35-36.

[14]Tall Stories: The Rise and Triumph of the Great American Whopper (New York: Funk & Wagnalls, 1931; rpt. New York: Harvest House, 1945), p. 157.

[15]Randolph, p. 199.

[16]Welsch, p. 28.

[17]See Welsch, p. 32.

[18]Tales of Old Time Texas (Boston: Little, Brown, 1955), p. 103, source attribution p. 321.

[19]"Paul Bunyan: Oil Man" in Follow de Drinkin' Gou'd, Publications of the Texas Folklore Society, No. 7 (Austin: University of Texas Press, 1928), p. 53.

[20]Welsch, p. 20

Bibliography

Barrick, Mac E. "Folktales from the Institute at
Duke." North Carolina Folklore Journal, 23,
(1975), 75-81.

Baughman, Ernest W. Type and Motif-Index of the
Folktales of England and North America. The
Hague, The Netherlands: Mouton & Co. Indiana
University Folklore Series, No. 20. 1966.

Boatright, Mody C. Folk Laughter on the American
Frontier. New York: Macmillan, 1949.

Brooks, John Lee. "Paul Bunyan: Oil Man." In Follow
de Drinkin' Gou'd. Austin: University of
Texas Press. Publications of the Texas Folklore
Society, No. 7 (1928), pp. 45-54.

Brunvand, Jan Harold. "The Hat-in-Mud Tale." In The
Sunny Slopes of Long Ago. Dallas: Southern
Methodist University Press. Publications of
the Texas Folklore Society, No. 33 (1966), pp.
100-109.

Dobie, J. Frank. Tales of Old-Time Texas. Boston:
Little, Brown, 1955.

Dorson, Richard M. Buying the Wind: Regional Folklore
in the United States. Chicago: University of
Chicago Press, 1964.

Hoig, Stan. The Humor of the American Cowboy. Caldwell,

Idaho: Caxton Press, 1958; paperback ed.
New York: Signet, 1960.

Lunt, C. Richard K. "Jones Tracy, Tall-Tale Hero from
Mount Desert Island." Northeast Folklore, 10
(1968), 1-75.

Randolph, Vance. We Always Lie To Strangers: Tall
Tales from the Ozarks. New York: Columbia
University Press, 1951.

Thomas, Lowell. Tall Stories: The Rise and Triumph
of the Great American Whopper. New York:
Funk & Wagnalls, 1931; New York: Harvest House
ed., 1945.

Welsch, Roger L. Shingling the Fog and Other Plains
Lies. Chicago: Swallow Press, 1972.

Glossary

The definitions that follow include general terms common in folklore studies.

archive—any depository for collected folklore, usually containing mainly "texts" of verbal lore but possibly also photographs, drawings, artifacts, and so on arranged by types, informants, regions, or collectors.

ballad—a folksong in stanzas that tells a story.

Child ballad—any of the 305 narrative folksongs included by Francis James Child in *The English and Scottish Popular Ballads* (1882–1898); frequently referred to by its "Child number."

context—the setting, situation, and audience response for the performance in tradition of any folklore item.

ethnomusicology—the specialized study of traditional music. Other such terms for similar studies include "ethnocuisine" for research in foodways and "ethnofolkloristics" for research in the traditions of folklorists.

fairy tale—the lay term for European wonder tales, nursery tales, magic tales, or *Märchen*, as they are variously called. The last term (see below) is preferred by folklorists, since few of these tales are about fairies, and since some literary stories, such as Hans Christian Andersen's, are also called "fairy tales."

fakelore—imitation folklore made up by writers and published with the claim that it is the real thing. Most Paul Bunyan stories are fakelore.

Finnish method—see *historic-geographic method*.

folk group—any group that has shared traditions of language, lore, customs, and so on. Such groups usually have been distinguished on the basis of such features as nationality, region, race, religion, occupation, or age.

o k hero—a personality, either historical or fictional, living or dead, about whom a cycle of traditional stories circulates; may or may not be a totally admirable figure.

folklife—the sum total of traditional aspects of a culture with particular reference to material and customary traditions rather than the verbal aspects of folk*lore*.

folklore—coined in 1846 to replace "popular antiquities" as a term referring to cultural survivals found in peasant traditions. The term was long applied only to "oral tradition," but then it expanded to include material culture or "folklife" and is now undergoing redefinition among scholars so as to take in the whole range of communicative events structured and transmitted according to traditional practices. In the popular mind "folklore" refers more generally to any folksy old-fashioned matters, and even more broadly often to error and misconception.

folksong revival—the widespread popularizing in recent decades— chiefly the 1950s to early 1960s—through professional singers and groups, concerts, and the mass media, of music that was or purported to be folk music.

historic-geographic method—a methodology developed by northern

European folk narrative scholars around the turn of the century for the comparative study of folktales in order to determine their probable archetypal forms, paths of diffusion, and kinds of variation. Sometimes called the "Finnish method," it was later applied to other genres of folklore but at present is not widely practiced.

informant—the human source of collected folklore, a long-accepted designation criticized recently for dehumanizing members of "the folk" whose living traditions are the folklorist's data.

Märchen—German term preferred by folklorists for the Indo-European folk narratives popularly called "fairy tales" (see above).

monogenesis—see *polygenesis*.

morphology—the essential form or structure of an item of folklore; also the study of these patterns.

motif—in Stith Thompson's system, any striking or unusual detail of a folk narrative, whether character, object, concept, formula, or other; catalogued and numbered in Thompson's six-volume *Motif-Index of Folk Literature* (rev. ed. 1955–1958) and widely used for archiving, annotating, and locating parallels for folk narratives.

motifeme—Alan Dundes's term for the structural units into which folk narratives may be divided by means of morphological analysis.

myth—the sacred traditional narratives of a culture, charters for belief, and validations of ritual. As used by literary critics, the term suggests broad symbolic themes usually embodied in metaphors; to the layperson, it often connotes popular misconceptions.

oikotype—a subtype of an item of folklore (usually a folktale) characteristic of a particular region.

polygenesis—the possibility of independent invention of similar themes or patterns in folk tradition, as opposed to "monogenesis," or the single origin of themes that are spread by diffusion.

popular culture—the standardized products and attitudes of mass manufacture and mass-media dissemination, as opposed to the innovative artistic products of "academic" or "high" culture and the traditional conservative products of "folk" culture.

text—the verbatim record of an item of verbal folklore, uncensored and unedited; the raw data for many folklore studies.

transcription—the task of rendering in graphic form—writing or musical notation—sound recordings of folklore performances.

type—a single Indo-European folktale plot as summarized and numbered in Antti Aarne's and Stith Thompson's *The Types of the Folktale* (rev. ed. 1961); sometimes called "tale type" or "AT Type" and generally referred to with its type-index number, as "Type 901, *The Taming of the Shrew.*"

variant—often synonymous with "text" (see above) or "version"; any record of a separate performance of a folklore item. The implication, however, is that a "variant" displays some difference from the supposed norm for that item.

Index of Authors